Damaged Like Me

Essays on Love, Harm, and Transformation

Damaged Like Me

Essays on Love, Harm, and Transformation

Kimberly Dark

Damaged Like Me: Essays on Love, Harm, and Transformation

© 2021 Kimberly Dark

This edition © 2021, AK Press (Chico/Edinburgh)

ISBN: 978-1-84935-414-1
E-ISBN: 978-1-84935-415-8
Library of Congress Control Number: 2020946142

AK Press	AK Press
370 Ryan Ave. #100	33 Tower St.
Chico, CA 95973	Edinburgh EH6 7BN
USA	Scotland
www.akpress.org	www.akuk.com
akpress@akpress.org	akuk@akpress.org

The above addresses would be delighted to provide you with the latest AK Press distribution catalog, which features books, pamphlets, zines, and stylish apparel published and/or distributed by AK Press. Alternatively, visit our websites for the complete catalog, latest news, and secure ordering.

"*When Does Life Begin?* It's the Wrong Question" first appeared as "Men Have Never Listened" in *Human Parts*, May 2019.
"I'm Not the Only One Who Lost Faith" first appeared in *Ravishly*, February, 2017.
"Fat Pedagogy in the Yoga Studio" first appeared in *Yoga, The Body, and Embodied Social Change,* eds. Beth Berila, Melanie Klein, Chelsea Jackson Roberts, Rowman & Littlefield, 2016.
"Unlovable" first appeared in *Full Grown People*, September 2016.
"I Said 'No' in Three Languages" first appeared in *Stir Journal*, September 2016.
"Trigger Warnings and the Myth of Oversensitive Students" first appeared in *Bullshitist*, September 2016.
"Three, Two, One" first appeared in *Full Grown People*, May 2016.
"Two A.M." first appeared in *Full Grown People*, March 2016.
"The Scholar-Performer and the Audience" first appeared in *Performing Scholartistry*, eds. Ardra Linette Cole, and Robyn Ann Ewing, Backalong Books, 2014.

Cover design by Toni Le Busque
Printed in the USA

This book is dedicated to reinvention. Often, we follow someone else's light to freedom, and maybe later we learn to lift a light for others—not for personal gain, nor to be better than somebody, but to show that certain strange paths stretch into the future too. There are gifts to share. No one is beyond love.

When language—whether printed or spoken or lived—is put to difficult or confusing experiences, we're not just reinventing ourselves. We enliven the culture that reaches both forward and back into other generations. Right now, we are somewhere in the past, saving our grandparents' lives. We are somewhere in the future saying thank you to ourselves, even as we turn to look further into what cannot yet be known.

CONTENTS

Introduction   1

1.   Damaged, Like Me   25
2.   Bodies in Motion   39
3.   I Said "No" in Three Languages   45
4.   How to Become a Racist Anti-Racism Educator   57
5.   Mothers and Misfires   65
6.   Two A.M.   71
7.   Trigger Warnings and the Myth of Oversensitive Students   77
8.   Unlovable   83
9.   The Body Politic   89
10.   Butch Dykes and Macho Men   101
11.   No Grammar Police, but Maybe a League
       of Language Altruists   105
12.   How We Come to Do It to Each Other   115
13.   Fat Pedagogy in the Yoga Class   123
14.   Language, Queer History, and Misogyny   139
15.   Three, Two, One   155
16.   Tattoos as Thresholds   167
17.   Letting the Body Lead   173
18.   The Body Is No Fickle Machine   181
19.   I'm Not the Only One Who Lost Faith   189
20.   *When Does Life Begin?* It's the Wrong Question   195
21.   At Least I'm a Thoughtful Liar   205
22.   Your Fruit Bowl Is (Reasonably) Safe   217
23.   The Scholar-Performer and the Audience   223
24.   Damaged, Like My Son   227

References   233

"I want the freedom to carve and chisel my own face, to staunch the bleeding with ashes, to fashion my own gods out of my entrails." —Gloria Anzaldua

"Language takes us to the bigness of ourselves, our origins, our universe.
    We choose our *kuleana*. I make sure that whoever comes into our learning, we give them a safe space to learn and we also hold them accountable." —Kumu Leialoha Ilae-Kaleimamahu

"Love is a combination of care, commitment, knowledge, responsibility, respect and trust." —bell hooks

"Optimism is a strategy for making a better future. Because unless you believe that the future can be better, you are unlikely to step up and take responsibility for making it so." —Noam Chomsky

INTRODUCTION

"I'm sometimes asked when will there be enough [women on the Supreme Court]? And I say 'When there are nine.' People are shocked. But there'd been nine men, and nobody's ever raised a question about that."

—Ruth Bader Ginsberg, Supreme Court justice

It's not so much that we didn't know, as that we didn't acknowledge the meaning of what we knew.

That which is common comes to be seen as normal. Occasionally, someone points to an obvious fact that had been rendered invisible. Looking at a picture of U.S. presidents, for instance, it's possible to note that they're all men or that only one is a person of color. We've seen the picture of the presidents in our elementary school classrooms and in online memes and in our minds for our entire lives. And whether or not one agrees with the power of the office, with the dominion of its values, there is a broader message being delivered in its homogeneity. A true message that perpetuates itself silently in the image and loudly in language, both subtly and overtly in every micro-interaction of government, business, and religion: none but white men are truly welcome here.

The issue here is how we make meaning of what we see. If one believes—even passively or unconsciously—that women are inferior leaders or that people of color are inferior humans, then that lack of representation is actually desirable. That would be conscious bias. If one associates young Black men and women with crime, considering them

1

a constant potential source of violence, then punitive—and even violent—policing might make sense. Yes, humans can actually hold the values of human equality sacred in the abstract without acting to dismantle the systems and actions that support our deeper biases, comforts, and associations.

New meanings don't just suddenly come into being. At the moment chattel slavery was abolished in the United States, slaveholders did not suddenly change their views on the humanity of those they held in bondage. They were being politically forced to change a practice but not an ideology. Every generation of white people in the United States since then has navigated the meaning of equality parallel to the ideologies of white supremacy and what it means to "make" and hold wealth. We are a nation obsessed with the accumulation of wealth as a measure of intelligence, hard work, and fortitude, despite that accumulation always having relied on the theft of land and labor of Black and brown people. We used to know that we diminish the humanity of Black and brown people. Now we hide what we know from ourselves.

The widespread 2020 marches and demands to address police brutality had to prompt change, and, because of how capital has come to supersede the worth of some humans, property damage was probably also needed before individuals and the systems that represent them were capable of hearing. Time will tell whether the positive changes in policing catalyzed by the events following George Floyd's death will hold or be transformed, as in the past, into new policies that enforce longstanding U.S. values. At this writing, abolition and a redistribution of resources toward true community safety have not been adequately explored. The old scripts—about who is worthy, intelligent, capable—stay with us for generations. We install new meanings in the culture through stories, through listening, through shared experiences, and by becoming significant in one another's lives. Massive public outcry and the amplification of marginalized voices can help us to listen and pay attention.

To anyone paying attention, it has also been obvious, ignored, and completely wrong that so many children are abused and that so many women are sexually assaulted, threatened, harassed, and marginalized. White supremacy, gender nonconformity, and the daily, persistent ridicule and dismissal of fat and disabled bodies are still difficult to discuss socially. We know, but we don't want to acknowledge what we know. Studies abound showing that people of color, fat people, women, and disabled people all suffer biases in the workplace, in law, in education, and in healthcare. Yet these biases persist because we don't discuss them publicly and we don't sanction the perpetrators of abuse on a regular basis. Few openly believe that child abuse and rape are okay and should not be stopped and addressed Yet the patterns in the data on how we punish those crimes show very different and distinct cultural values. The fact that we do not actually focus on stopping abusers and addressing their actions as part of communities that deserve safety and care shows that the culture is not interested in disturbing male dominion.

The #metoo movement has propelled conversations about sexual assault into broader contexts much as the recent Black Lives Matter protests have increased conversations about police brutality. My stepmother, in her seventies, used the #metoo movement as a time to disclose her own experiences with sexual assault, on social media. I've been writing and speaking about these topics for years, and, though she's been interested in my work, it wasn't enough to prompt her disclosure. She came forward because a public conversation had progressed to the point where solidarity and bravery, rather than fear, prevailed.

Progress is hard because we snap back to what comforts us—or at least what's familiar—like tight little rubber bands. However, maybe it's possible for greater elasticity to emerge at the intersections of supremacist issues, and for daily, individual practices with language and interaction to encourage lasting change.

Culture is shifting in multiple directions at once with regard to revelations about how white men have organized human systems to their benefit for generations. Those men with fewer financial resources find it difficult to discern their privilege and too readily become foot soldiers in the war to maintain the status quo of resource distribution. This paradox doesn't reveal those men as idiots; it shows how deeply attached to identity we are, as humans. Identification with white supremacist values is on the rise. As the gap between rich and poor has widened in the United States (as a result of social policies, not the "natural order" of capitalism), discussions about appearance/identity privilege become quickly contentious. Yet harbingers of change like Alexandra Ocasio-Cortez are becoming public figures and making a claim to long-held power structures. Much maligned and resilient, she is showing she's not afraid of hard work and learning. Some don't hesitate to say that because she is young, or female or Latinx that she knows and can do nothing. Clearly, this is also profoundly and completely wrong. In addition to being capable of ignoring the obvious, we are also capable of stating the opposite of truth as fact.

So, with an understanding that marginalized and traumatized people, together, are a large cultural majority who have often been barred from leadership by stories and assumptions, what will we do?

I suggest we find ways to re-story public discourse so that we can see more possibilities and enact them. The very existence of young women of color in public leadership roles is doing exactly this. Whether we are discussing Alexandra Ocasio-Cortez, Alicia Garza, Stacy Abrams, Patrisse Cullors, or any other variety of public leaders whose roles vary widely, we are receiving a message, in their public labors, that can help re-story public possibility. We need more ways to understand full participation—in media and the creation of knowledge and the framing of our very thinking and feeling. We can leverage the telling of individual stories into the transformation of culture more consciously than has ever occurred before because of the speed of discussion across electronic media. And still, much of how we learn boils down to daily interactions, how we tell others about our lives as they happen, and how they are heard, understood, and acted upon. We make meaning on our own and in concert. The closer we come to sharing experiences rather than just interpretations, the better.

My experiences as an incest survivor, as a fat queer woman, and as an active cultural creator—not just a cultural critic—have given me a kind of training and expertise that is valuable. I'm also trained, as a sociologist, to see and investigate social patterns. For so long, and even now, people like me (and likely you, for some specific reasons which you may believe you should hide) have been dismissed as biased about the exact topics on which we are expert. Of course, in the moment of fear or trauma or abuse, an individual is not empowered and can do little to contribute and improve society. The assumption that a person can never integrate and understand these experiences is incorrect, however. The assumption that those who are "damaged" are of no use is a nefarious silencer.

We must keep moving out into broader spheres of society and improving our world for the better. We take up credibility as it's due and use our skills of re-creation to phoenix the culture from the ashes of trauma and stale expectations. We apply new thought frameworks and use more of our knowledge—particularly our body wisdom, so long thought to impede "rational" thought. The intuition that helped us to survive, that made us capable of observing and understanding others in order to avert danger, will help us create a more viable and compassionate culture for all.

I'm prompting new ways of seeing familiar things, through storytelling. I'm suggesting that you find pleasure in these stories and in your body and abilities. Especially when your body has been maligned and your experiences may have been anything but pleasurable. I'm also suggesting that you consider how you come to love, how you allow yourself to be loved. This is no small part of the cultural revolution we can enact. We have to learn to love bodies and lives we were taught were not respectable—including our own. It's time to embrace the gifts you've developed in response to the life you've lived and to give those gifts boldly. Society needs them.

Mental Frameworks and Emotional Attachments

My female friend has been a firefighter for more than twenty years, and women in the fire service are pretty scarce. Even now, fewer than 3 percent of all firefighters in the United States are women. Many develop an interest in the profession because they have male family members who are firefighters—uncles, brothers, and fathers who encourage them and lend their credibility to the woman's pursuit. Many are also big, strong women; many are gender-nonconforming in subtle or overt ways. There aren't so many girly-girls on the job.

It's easy to say, Whoa, of course not. Because that's a man's job. A firefighter has to be able to carry someone out of a burning building!

When that image pops to mind, is it a man carrying a child or a petite woman?

We build reality from the images we've grown up with. And we innovate. It helps to acknowledge how inherent some images have become. The best firefighters in our cultural imagination are men. They're pulling heavy hose; they're scaling heavy wooden ladders. The vast majority of women can't do that kind of work. What are those feminists thinking?

After touring a fire station in Holland, I learned, once again, that cultural context can shift perspective. Lightweight aluminum ladders are the norm in First World fire stations, technology and teamwork assist in the heavy lifting, and body-size diversity is actually a boon in tight rescue situations.

My friend was an advocate for women in the fire service. After a long career of pointing out overt sexism in a male-dominated profession, she started a girl's fire camp. Being big and strong herself, she saw how women struggled with upper body strength and taught them to use both leg and arm muscles to greater efficiency to pass the physical exams. She networked with other female firefighters and remained aware of her union-won rights to things like a gender-appropriate shower and changing room. One station where she worked back in the 1990s had to add on to the building to provide such a facility. She (and her union) rejected the original assumption that she should go across the street to use another city facility to change clothes.

The year she and I visited Amsterdam on vacation, we met up with two women she'd come to know through a Women in the Fire Service conference. They were firefighters too and arranged a tour of their fire station. Delighted to show us around, they also commented on how odd they found gender assumptions in U.S. fire stations. They marveled at how, in the United States, the image of hulking, masculine strength still prevailed as a professional standard—an image that largely excludes women. To be clear, there is not gender parity in the Dutch fire service, but it's better than in the United States.

They showed us equipment and discussed procedures. While fighting fire was also frequently a familial profession in Holland, it wasn't so strange for women to join the fire service. They shrugged and said, "Well, we use research, best practice, and good equipment to get the job done." Their systems are often superior and require firefighters to be strong and capable but not Herculean.

Superficially, it seems that every fire service in the world has the same goal. Fire fighters fight fire. The cultural assumptions that undergird that simple truth tell a different story. In the United States, firefighters are part of a public distress response team that attends to both medical and fire emergencies. Most calls in urban areas are medical calls. A small percentage deal with fire. Yet we rarely see the big red engine and think of medical emergencies. The color and size of the truck itself invokes meaning. Public images of firefighters usually depict men rescuing children (and, interestingly, pets) from peril. Big men guard what families value.

After the World Trade Center buildings fell in New York on September 11, 2001, the role of firefighters as rescuers was further solidified. A new aspect of the professional image emerged as well—upholder of patriotic values. Suddenly, the U.S. flag became part of every image of firefighters. Previously, the job had community-hero connotations. Now, community and country became inextricably linked. In so many ways, the profession connotes masculinity. No wonder it's hard to just invite women to apply for the job, tell the men to welcome them, and think the work of gender integration is done.

Among firefighters in Holland, the Dutch cultural values of teamwork, equity, and use of modern technology were visible in procedures, images, and interactions. Decisions were based more on research than on tradition, as in the United States. With different underlying patterns in the organization of the work, different processes seem logical. In the

United States, ours is a deeply gendered system. Traditionally feminine methods of communication, feminine bodies, and women's approaches are not valued in the U.S. fire service. The literature on women in the fire service often cites ill-fitting safety gear as a significant challenge. So strong is the masculine standard that simply redesigning clothing for different bodies seems like an insurmountable barrier. Women who successfully acculturate must meet masculine standards and take on the traditional values of the profession.

Patterns across Themes

Simple, linear stories are not enough if we truly want to understand how we've created and maintained the problems we face as a society. We need complex stories that reveal the architecture of everyday life—the things we've hidden from ourselves as "simple" and "true."

In the United States, we're particularly limited in our ability to see "reality" in terms of cultural context because so few of us travel abroad, or, when we do so, it's for short recreational trips rather than actually exploring another culture for learning or in collegial relationships.

In the fire service example, it can seem absurd for a city to spend the additional funds to build women's showers and changing facilities or to redesign safety gear with differently proportioned bodies in mind. After all, the numbers of female firefighters are so small and the benefit to the city seems tiny. It's easy to see why the men who work in those stations feel they're being asked to change their habits and compromise their comfort for no good reason. Yet the specific efforts and barriers to include women into male-dominated professions invoke patterns that replicate across all forms of oppression. If we focus on individual stories about fire stations—or even individual stories about gender, we may miss the broader landscape of how privilege and oppression work in everyday life.

Each of the essays in this collection tells a specific stand-alone story about my life, my cultural context, and how the two intersect. Many of them reveal, through detail and specificity, the architecture of everyday life—in both public and very private settings. They reveal the fact that we are all powerful social creators. Indeed, every part of human culture was created by humans. We either re-create or re-inscribe culture day by day through our words, interactions, what we allow, and what we negate.

There's something more. As a collection, these essays begin to offer a map for a cultural terrain that may be in constant flux but is nonetheless understandable for the evolving landscape that it is. Ideally, each person's individual body-mind-life map would contribute to our cultural understanding. Currently, only certain socially sanctioned stories are allowed to be part of the broader cultural map. Even those who believe in the value of diversity as an abstract concept can't easily see how to bring those values into action given the powerful longevity of often-invisible institutions such as sexism, racism, classism, and sizeism.

These essays are about how social norms and patterns are established and disrupted again and again. They acknowledge the multiplicity of human roles and behaviors. Every social ill, power, and possibility lives in each individual. Yes, the essays are, at turns, funny and tragic, surprising and hopeful. And together they offer a model for reclaiming the conscious ability to create culture. We are indeed cultural creators, whether we do so passively or actively.

You may feel at times like you're reading memoir and, at turns, cultural analysis. These narratives are connected through the concept of "damage"—how we come to be seen as less than. Sometimes these stories involve trauma—both overt trauma like incest and the sort of everyday cumulative trauma that makes much of the world feel like a hostile environment for some, even though others seem to be operating with ease. These essays are connected via the patterns they reveal across seemingly unconnected approaches and themes. These patterns exist a little differently in every life. A complex story is not necessarily a messy story. Many of the ways people are damaged, uplifted, vexed, find joy, et cetera. follow patterns. The world is full of complex and repeating patterns; pleasure guides us toward understanding.

Your life is neither random nor predictable. It's a complex map, and you can't pretend that certain locations don't exist—though you can do your best to keep from traveling rough terrain repeatedly. You can't poke out holes in the map of your life as if you're making a paper snowflake, something prettier than the original experiences. We are more than our simple, publicly shared stories suggest. The lives we've led form the ways we see the world. Each human map holds secrets to help us navigate the depths of love and loss, anger, fear, and every human emotion and trait possible, colored exactly the hue of individual sovereignty.

The simple point A to point B story, even with a little flourish or subplot, does not serve our common wisdom in the same way that complexity serves us. Creativity gives us endless new views on our own maps, and, little by little, we start to understand how our landscapes might match up with others. We can do this consciously but only if we're somewhat aware of what we bring to the group. Every map is damaged. Every one. The circumstances of this world damage all of us. If you believe you're navigating the cultural terrain without being hurt by violence, including the violence done to others, then you are surely damaged by your own isolation. Most people could stand to improve their capacity to look into others eyes and listen, just listen, until it hurts.

I want you to know that your story doesn't have to conform to other's stories. We become relevant to one another through our specificity and the oscillating patterns we create across issues and groups.

Damage

You probably already know the unwritten rules about who is allowed to be the author of cultural stories.

Or maybe you don't.

Social conditioning about who's allowed to speak and not speak is powerful enough that often it seems as though a range of stories are being heard. Or, even stranger, it can seem that marginalized stories are actually taking up more space in public discourse than "mainstream" stories. For instance, the story about female firefighters may, if it's new to you, take up an irritating (or thrilling) residence in your thinking, and for months you may feel that you "just read" that story. However, what you've read and seen about firefighters from week to week during that time is likely to focus on men and on stories that fit familiar cultural patterns. They are not remarkable, nor do they stand out, especially if they give you a comfortable or patriotic or pleasurable feeling. The story about the female firefighters and their ill-fitting safety suits and their oddly masculine pursuits—that story stands out. So it seems that female firefighters dominate the news.

Minds have certain habits. In "confirmation bias" we try to confirm whatever patterns we've already come to recognize. Most of us can remember buying a car and suddenly seeing that car everywhere. Or becoming a parent and starting to think there's a new population boom. It's not that reality has suddenly bent to your experience but that you are experiencing a certain part of reality vibrantly. You recognize a thing; the mind normalizes it; it's comfortable to see it. This is how some people suddenly believe that because the president was African American, African Americans as a group are in leadership positions all over the country. (Spoiler: they are not.)

Another habit of mind is to become fatigued by positive change efforts that seem "too big" or somehow "too difficult." For instance, it's common for people to talk about the horrors of sexism in other countries or in past time periods. The topic is allowed discursive space; it's not as though people are denying the problem of harassment, assault, and subjugation of women. They are simply placing their awareness of sexism outside of their immediate environments. They are blind to how they participate as perpetrators, victims, and bystanders. We can even celebrate the end of a problem as it is worsening, as in the case of school integration in the United States. The end of legally enforced racial segregation did not change the circumstance of racial segregation for the vast majority of people. Decades after "schools were integrated" in the United States, few discuss the fact that racial segregation is actually the norm in schools and housing, not the exception.

Luckily, empirical evidence can rescue us from errors of perception. It's actually possible to know how many times gender was referenced with regard to firefighting in a given period and what those references were. There isn't data about everything, but there's a lot of data. It's possible to know what percentage of African American students finish an undergraduate degree, what percentage of university professors are Latinx or transgender or come from poverty. We can know what percentage of plays written by women were professionally produced in the United States and how that figure has risen and fallen over the past twenty years. Data is available on representation of certain voices in specific roles—more than enough to start meaningful discussions about how narrow our public representation of stories actually are.

Then there's the matter of who can discuss which topics and how. What language can an individual use and from what position? In professional settings, it's often important to be seen as a person with no problems, completely in control of oneself, and certainly showing human emotion is not tolerated. For instance, a therapist who specializes in eating disorders, and who has survived and/or recovered from an eating disorder, is likely to highlight only his academic position and expertise when speaking about eating disorders. Personal knowledge is considered inferior, inappropriate, or even detrimental to being taken seriously. And if one does "come out" regarding such a status, there must never be discussion about how traumatic experiences influence one's life in an ongoing way.

Anyone who has been underprivileged by existing hierarchies is seen as "damaged" and therefore not a viable contributor to broader cultural understanding. We must only show the "respectable" parts of ourselves. Victimhood, for some, is even less respectable than having been a perpetrator. Think about boys on sports teams who are seen as "having gone too far" if they rape, whereas those they victimize are admitting having been dominated or humiliated. Culturally, we hold greater disdain for the second position than for the first. Those who are "damaged" by abuse seem worthy of dismissal—a self-fulfilling prophecy by which the abused deserve more abuse. Further, perpetrators of abuse are never allowed to acknowledge their own humanity, show remorse, and experience the depth of love possible in interconnectedness.

Why does conformity to "respectable" social narratives seem so important?

It's simple, really. In a society based on competition and profit, we manage our identities to greatest gain. It's what we learn as children and in every aspect of human culture. Sociologist Erving Goffman explained it to us back in the 1950s. We conceal or diminish our stigmatized identities so that others don't see us as damaged goods. If you're fat, you try to look thin. If you're poor, you try to look middle class. Think about the female firefighter's conundrum regarding gender conformity. Women who are gender-conforming receive greater social privilege than those who "look like men" in attire and comportment. Yet the work itself and the physicality it requires are counter to the pursuit of femininity. By definition, in a "male" profession, female firefighters are wearing men's clothes. It's a tricky transformation. Be big and strong but not manly. Inspire confidence and admiration but without seeming like a man. Women's sports teams face a similar problem. In order to increase the popularity of women's sports, teams often hire stylists for photo shoots to create the feminine image that the players lack on the field when engaged in competition.

Abuse is trickier still to discuss. It would seem that abusers—the ones whose behavior the culture has criminalized—would be the stigmatized parties. And, again, empirical evidence says otherwise. Many men who use threats and violence remain respectable, whereas people of all genders who discuss harassment or abuse become personally suspect. They're immediately assumed to be irreparably broken by their experiences, angry, and biased on any topic related to the abuse, the abuser, or their own experiences. Consider how Dr. Blasey-Ford's family had to move, fleeing death threats, after she came forward to assert that Supreme Court Justice Kavanaugh had assaulted her. Not only were her allegations not taken seriously by those with power, she was vilified to the point where individuals threatened harm and murder. Though many, seeking to see things fairly, believed that her word against his felt tricky to decide, she is the one whose life was threatened for speaking her word. Similarly, people who speak up about racism are said to be "playing the race card" though there's empirical evidence that it's one of the least valuable cards to throw onto the table, because of stigma.

Certain bodies become the receptacle for cultural shame about the abuses perpetuated on those bodies. Women's bodies are the social location for discussions on gender, on rape, on domestic violence. Even though other genders experience sexual violence and domestic abuse too, somehow women are seen as biased in discussing gender, whereas men aren't. Both have gender. People of color are seen as biased when discussing race, whereas white people aren't. Both have race. Indeed, it can be argued that whiteness and maleness—as default categories—are actually the social locations within which one knows the least about race or gender because all social systems are built to accommodate them. The paradox of denying "isms" is that often, in order to do it, the deniers invoke the inferiority of the party being oppressed. Again, those who deny knowing the power of social hierarchies, and try to claim that society is basically fair, are aware of inequality, covered only by a thin veneer of social etiquette. Through denial, they blunt their own senses to the world around them.

We could, instead, begin to see those who have experienced stigmatized events as experts on those events. That's how it works with non-stigmatized eyewitness accounts. When a hurricane damages a coastline, news crews go directly to those who lived there, saw the storm coming, felt the rain. They're particularly interested in the human responses to having lost a home, protected a family, overcome challenges using ingenuity. We could do the same with abuse and harassment. There are a lot of ways to be expert. There are a lot of ways to be damaged. One can be damaged by the invisible habits of holding dominion, just as surely (though maybe not as painfully) as by overt repression.

It's as simple as this. If you want to know about a certain type of oppression, you have to ask the person who is oppressed. The person who doesn't have that experience likely can't see the patterns—let alone the nuances—very clearly, if at all. Those who lack privilege have studied its absence intently. They've learned its contours, and sometimes they can extrapolate their knowledge to other systems of oppression. Sometimes not.

A white man who comes from poverty has witnessed how assumptions about poor people in our culture are damaging. People have thought him lazy or stupid just because he lacks wealth. It's as though wealth itself is a sign of ingenuity and hard work even though, empirically, we know it's not so. That man who may see so clearly down the road of class privilege may or may not be able to see that derisive views of people of color function in just the same way. Likely, that individual—without invested listening to people of other races—would not see racism. He may not even have turned to look down that other road because he's so consumed with figuring out how to navigate his own rough road, how to maximize the privileges he has. Those larger patterns remain invisible.

More troublingly, that man might even have tuned his attention to the cultural examples he sees of people in color in positions of power. Without considering that the Latinx mayor or the Korean movie director or the Black president are exceptions in their positions, he may even think people of color have more power and opportunity than people "like him." It's easier and easier for that man to find others who believe as he does—not only because the Internet has made it easier for those with fringe views easier to find one another. There are actually people with power and resources organizing others to believe in falsehoods for their own gains. Though it is easy enough to disprove the perception that "everywhere you look nowadays, people of color are in positions of power," it's possible that a person will hold and nurture falsehoods with communities of people who do the same.

Consistently, studies show that white people are more likely than people of color to say that racism is primarily in the past in the United States. A lot more likely. Empirically of course, racism is quantifiable, qualifiable, and a current lived experience among people who can give first-person accounts. Though it was traumatizing for many Black people to relive their stories of abuse and terror at the hands of police in 2020, their efforts punched through the membrane of apathy and misinformation in order to make political discussions and progress possible. To be sure, many white people remain insulated, never stepping onto the road toward knowing those who are racially different. Awareness and interest in knowing others can create habits of inquiry at any moment in each of our lives. At any moment, it's possible to turn away from knowing other's views too. Sometimes we are even rewarded for that turning away, so we must learn how to overcome that temptation.

Often, if a group of people experiences two or more types of oppression, they are more likely to be able to extrapolate those experiences to other groups. They're more likely to notice patterns across issues. They listen and observe more carefully beyond the categories we've all been taught. Or at least they are likely to consider close listening. It's certainly possible to be oppressed and oppress others. It's possible to build up a wall of fear around an awareness that threatens to blow your house down.

Love and proximity help too. That's why the quest for racial integration in the United States was significant and should not have been abandoned. When school integration efforts, such as bussing, were abandoned, many Americans felt relieved. It was uncomfortable and simply too hard. White parents didn't understand the gains their children were receiving—though many of us who experienced bussing to schools in neighborhoods we'd never seen know the importance of what we were given—even decades later. This lack of systemic and cultural understanding obscured the fact that policy makers didn't simply abandon those efforts like a curriculum experiment. Those efforts to link race and class were violently suppressed. Many Black Panthers and Black activists were murdered and jailed. Martin Luther King Jr. also knew that the attempt to link race with class for social betterment was an effort that he might not survive. He was right, and many never fully understood the value of the efforts that these people attempted and that the U.S. government violently suppressed. This fatigue with attempting fairness is precisely why we need leaders who help us stay with efforts such as class analysis and racial integration.

There is a magic in proximity. We need to see those whom we

perceive as different as being also the same in significant, humanity-affirming ways. We need compassion, along with the ability to easily make friends, fall in love, and make families—actually integrate—with those whom we believe to be different.

Discussing Our Damage and Choosing Transformation

People who have experienced things that are difficult to discuss have important perspectives. Many have cultivated deep wisdom as they navigate the rough waters of public opinion while reconstructing their lives. It's a bit like building the boat you're steering, while at sea—and in the middle of a storm. Humans are so astonishingly capable of reinvention that this is actually possible.

Consider how many experiences we are supposed to absorb into ourselves and not discuss: violence, verbal abuse, incarceration, mental illness, discrimination, exile, harassment, immigration, homelessness, and, most especially, experiences related to sexual abuse of power: rape, incest, unwanted sexual contact of any kind. We are all damaged—perpetrators, victims, and bystanders. Those labeled as victims become the social location for understanding damage. The rest believe they can visit that place at will, intellectually, as observers, but don't have to live there. But we all live in a world built by patterns of abuse and dominion and defined by damage. We live in a world full of hope, resiliency, and ingenuity as well. We are vulnerable, and the ability to harm and be harmed is in each of us. Imagine how it would be if those who have harmed others could be heard and understood. Especially in their remorseful complexity. We each share DNA and experiences and popular culture with people who do horrific things. Their humanity is ours as well.

The more stigmatized a position is, the more difficult it is to claim it as a platform of knowledge. I am damaged. You are damaged. I suggest you claim every bit of expertise in your body-mind-life. The culture needs you.

Luckily, the veneer of social hierarchy is cracking, but it's not broken yet. There are more people saying no, I won't carry shame about having been raped. No. Racism organizes our lives every day; black lives matter. No, you can't keep me out of the bathroom because my appearance and choices frighten you. No, I won't refuse to swim because I don't have "a bikini body." Every body deserves pleasure.

The more people begin to speak from "damage," the more we practice respecting the diversity of one another's experiences, the more we heal each other and become able to transform culture. Rather than needing to build the boat on the stormy sea, the sea calms a bit. The next generation inherits greater building skills. Fewer people accept the illusion that human respectability should exclude some and elevate others. I am telling you that every time you build grace from pain, you serve the common good. You are an expert. You can be a guide. You are worthy of compassionate attention.

Black feminist thinkers have guided my scholarly work. I rarely get into bed at night without having discussed Erving Goffman's ideas about identity management somehow. There are others. But women-of-color feminists? Scholars and artists? I am grateful to them beyond measure. Alice Walker, Angela Davis, Audre Lorde, bell hooks, Gloria Anzaldua, Maya Angelou, Patricia Hill Collins, Zora Neale Hurston… I could go on. They have helped to make and remake me. They invited me into a broader landscape than I was given. They expand my map and help to put some of my more painful neighborhoods into a broader context. Over the years, I've been asked why I would choose scholarly mentors so different from myself. As a young person with scholarly "potential," the assumption seemed to be that I should seek to be more kindred with the white male scholars in the traditional canon of social science. What an odd perspective, really, when I had none of their influence and experience. The assumption also, when we ask thinkers why they have "fringe" interests, is that everyone should be interested in the mainstream. Everyone should be interested in the thoughts and writings of white, Western European or American men.

There are so many moments in which we are asked to choose sides. I acknowledge that some of me is on all the sides. I know that this acknowledgement is likely more difficult for those who have greater material investment in inequality (whether or not they are actually receiving full benefits of that investment). The very concept of "sides" shows the dangerously dichotomous thinking that pervades our culture, and while shifting that thinking doesn't automatically shift investment, it can help. I have some privileged identities and some not privileged identities. That's true for most, and most of us realized it because of suffering—either our own or our beloveds'. We have to keep looking for what we don't know. Sometimes, we'll be able to see traditional thinkers and culture makers as "our own" though we have little in common with them. Or we'll hold up different commonalities, as when I chose to read more bell hooks and less Émile Durkheim. Others need to seek out diverse views in order to challenge the assumption that they could be considered complete without them. Though I am queer and fat and female and an incest survivor, et cetera, I need to keep unfolding my understanding of the world and humbly offering to connect my map to others. That's how we expand our abilities. I want to see down as many roads as the world offers me so that I die with more understanding and peace than I had as a child. I will die having helped others. It's a simple, selfish, benevolent goal.

The essays in this collection offer specific, nuanced stories of social damage, disruption of norms and values about what it means to be a target for social damage. I'm offering you what we rarely receive in U.S. culture—so fixated are we on "doing it ourselves." I'm offering you my map, my stories, examples, models for communication, experiments in self-love. I intend to give you something to cry about and something to feel hopeful about, all in the same essay. I want to remind you that we are creating the world, even as it creates us. We can re-create ourselves too. That's how the world changes.

The Hero's Journey—and What the Rest of Us Can Make Together

Part of why we're so attached to the cultural image of the big strong man carrying the child out of the burning building is that we can identify with both the hero and the child. Sometimes we need rescuing.

Sometimes we face adversity, feel nearly broken, build strength, and then overcome. The hero's journey, as described by Joseph Campbell, is a quintessentially masculine Western archetype. It's easy to forget that there are more people in every story than can be shown in the image on the book jacket.

Having occasional stories told from alternate perspectives is not enough to prompt cultural transformation. Whenever there is a narrative and a counter-narrative, dichotomy is reinforced. Dualism remains the norm. Sometimes it seems radical enough to tell the heroine's story once in a while, or to elevate individuals with identities and appearances that are not normally visible in public to hero status. It's not enough. Complexity within *each* story is what helps us break the spell of binary constructions and remember that the collective map we are creating can lead us to cultural transformation.

Simply challenging a norm with exceptions allows hierarchical institutions to remain intact. Change becomes possible when we re-analyze, through our own complexity and empirical social patterns, the systems that maintain expectations (and allow exceptions). My task is not just to tell an alternative story but also to reveal the complex patterns that emerge and how they might inform the re-creation of systems that create reality. We are capable of building the boat while sailing it—such is our relationship to human culture. Once the storm of judgment and abuse calms, it becomes so much easier. So resilient, so capable are humans, despite our never-ending flaws and personal insurrections.

Alternative narratives often follow a pattern that doesn't allow complexity, just like the hero's journey follows a pattern. Because stories of stigmatized identity are hard to tell, they're often distilled into easily digestible narratives that begin in tragedy and end in hope and triumph. There's nothing wrong with those stories if they give someone the will to survive and persevere. And those stories fail to adequately complicate our human maps. Some of the landmarks are left out because they're inconvenient. We need more detail in the map for cultural transformation.

These are the linear stories people are accustomed to hearing about some of the themes I discuss.

Sexual orientation: I was confused, then closeted and miserable. I found courage/love/wisdom, and I came out. It was hard, but people respected me, and my self-respect grew. You should be courageous too. The End.

Body acceptance: I was sad and miserable. People bullied me. I found courage/love/wisdom and decided not to listen to the haters anymore. It was hard, but people respected me and my self-respect grew. You should be courageous too. The End.

Child abuse: I was in danger with nowhere to turn. I found courage/love/wisdom and decided to stop blaming myself and get help. It was hard, but people respected me and my self-respect grew. You should be courageous too. The End.

I could go on. Rewards come to those who persevere; hard work and community erase all hardships. There's more. We also have to acknowledge the ways in which we are the architects of our misery and how we sometimes perpetuate others' suffering too. We have to acknowledge the ways in which existing social systems support or thwart our individual efforts. Human culture is but/and, rather than either/or.

There is more to tell, and good reasons to fear complexity—at least superficially. We are afraid of confusion, afraid of tackling too many things at once without line-item veto. We're afraid that seeing too much complexity might diminish momentum toward a clear and just goal. We're afraid of stories that could push us under for too long without a breath or that could make us feel stupid.

Fair enough. I'm asking you to put aside those fears for a moment, find pleasure in these stories and consider that complexity is already a fact of living, whether you embrace it or not. As the tradition of Hawaiian ho'opono'pono tells us, love prevails over all trauma. Love does not prevent all trauma. Sometimes we have a rough road. Or we make a rough road. And then we realize it's possible to choose again. And again. Ad infinitum.

I focus on intersections of issues and experiences rather than on a discrete theme with a specific audience. I'm not interested in just writing funny, heartwarming stories about being a queer mom, though I have written those stories. I am not interested in telling the tale of growing up fat, breaking free of social stigma, and developing self-love, though I write those stories. The trouble with isolating these themes is that their simplicity fails to offer a bridge toward cultural transformation. These stories fail to illuminate why personal and social change remain difficult despite positive intentions.

Though the intersections of my identities, experiences, and views may feel surprising, I'm not that unique. Many people conceal certain identities and highlight others to the point where they forget that their narratives are actually more complex. They forget until they hear a story of complexity with which they relate. I've been writing and performing stories about complexity for decades. I know how eager people are to relate. What's unique is that I share my complexities. Part of what allows people to relate is recognizable intersections and the specificity of time and place. Yes, we each hold stereotypes about artists, about abuse survivors, about fat women, about parents, about scholars. I'm not just asking you to challenge those stereotypes in general, abstract terms. I'm holding a door open for you to know me, here and now, in the culture we share.

There are others like me. That is to say, there are others who are like me in exactly their own ways. No doubt, it's socially easier to make the seams between our identities disappear. And growing numbers of us are saying no, I will persist in my complexity for the common good. There are others who are breaking containers and pulling their mangled maps out in public, unfolding them at bus stops and asking friends to have a look. Some are throwing map images onto bedroom walls lit by candles, carving their maps into fallow cornfields, shining their maps like beacons onto distant planets, mixing their maps into thousand ingredient cocktails to be served on the verandah of slave-built mansions. Learning occurs at the point where disparate things start to become relatable and relate to oneself as well.

As an artist and a social scientist, I am the researcher and the independent variable. I pay attention, document the methodology, look for patterns, and also offer you this: the carefully constructed humor, pain, hope and brilliance of specificity. Follow the map of my body-mind-life stories. Then follow your own. Connect with others. Let's see where we can go.

1.

DAMAGED, LIKE ME

I.

I saw a porno snuff film for the first time in Las Vegas, more than thirty-five years ago. I was there recently for a professional conference, and the memory came back slowly. Which boyfriend was I with? Did I get up and leave? I know I didn't see the end.

I remember what shoes I was wearing during that snuff film. I loved them. So seventies, those shoes. A tall wedge heel with twisted jute wrapped around the whole platform, and then crossed over the vamp, with the leather—I don't think it was real leather—and my painted toenails poked out the little openings in front. Just three of them visible on each foot.

I know I didn't see the end of the film. I walked back out into the casino and got myself lost for a while. I remember looking down at my shoes and knowing I looked older than I was. No one would question me being in the casino. Or maybe they would. I couldn't speak for a while after leaving the film. Better keep moving. I got lost in the casino, ended up back in the hotel room.

That was no boyfriend I was with. It was my stepfather. And no one questioned my return to the hotel room because it's where I should've been in the first place, with my mother. I was eleven years old after all. I said I was twenty-two if anyone asked. Saying you're twenty-one, when you're lying, sounds suspicious. Like you just need to be old enough to drink. Twenty-two doesn't sound so amateur. I'd done the math and knew just what date I needed to be born to be twenty-two.

I lied to adults easily. I said I was older if I needed to be older. I said I was fine and everything was good when it was definitely not good. It's easier to say "everything's good" than to be pitied for everything being not good when you don't have the power to change things.

This is a story about how memory returns. It's a story about pornography. It's a story about dominion. "Why didn't she speak up sooner" is a popular question these days, with many women (and others) shaking loose memories of rape, assault, and moments with men when everything was definitely not good.

At eleven, I looked like I might have been twenty-two, if that's what I meant for you to believe. I spoke with confidence and an assured, upright sexy that people said I was born with. Well, I must've gotten it somewhere. That's what people said but often in moments when it sounded like they needed an excuse.

I wandered out of the room where the film was playing and walked through the casino, then back up to the hotel room. My stepfather came in a little while after me. My mother admonished him gently for leaving me alone, letting me walk back to the room by myself. I had told her he was on his way. I walked up just ahead of him while he finished gambling. I didn't say anything about that room full of mostly men, watching that film on a pull-down screen and his hot breath in my ear as the movie-woman took off her little jacket and laid it on the bed. The hot breath saying, "You know what happens in the end of this one, right? This is no regular porno. It's something new. I had to get a special invitation to be here."

She took off her dress and sat on the bed in underwear, long hair, just like mine, falling around her shoulders. I started looking around the room, realizing there were only a few bodies that looked like mine, that looked like the woman on the screen. I looked at the room on the screen, where the woman had become topless, roughly handled by the hairy-chested man. It looked like my room in that very hotel.

"After they do it, he kills her. It's not fake blood either, like a movie. I mean he really does it. Can you believe that?"

And, you know, I could.

You want this to be a simple story about a terrible incident. Of course you do. That will mean that you can feel a cathartic grief about it that positions you as a compassionate person on the right side of life's many moral divisions. You hope this story will ask nothing from you but your outrage, compassion, and maybe a feeling of inspiration that if I can overcome hardship, so can you. You do not wish for this to be a story that requires you to think of how your own memories have been shaped by social expectations, how social patterns are formed and how we accept and even expect certain terrible things to happen. You don't want to think about where you are standing in the scenarios I'm offering. You don't want to think about how you devalue certain stories even as you believe in the human dignity of all people.

I can't give you what you want. This is a story about how scenes are reconstructed when your body becomes a disaster site, an explosion, or more accurately, an implosion.

When they blow up those big Las Vegas casinos to make room for more modern big Las Vegas casinos, they implode the buildings so that business can go on all around, even while the destruction is happening. That hotel where my family stayed, where they showed that snuff film, isn't there anymore. I might've remembered if I'd walked into the lobby and seen my feet on the pattern of the carpet, but it's gone. Sometimes, we can take ourselves out of difficult circumstances, build our lives anew and forget. Sometimes we have to change details more actively in order to move on. Sometimes it takes something shocking to bring information back—like the face of someone who tried to rape you on television with the words "Supreme Court justice" underneath. And suddenly the fear is back and the profound sense of *this is not right* and *someone needs to do something*, and suddenly you realize you are someone.

I was in Las Vegas recently for a professional conference, and as I rode alone in the taxi toward the Strip, as the hotels came into view to my right, something in my memory came into focus. Maybe because I saw the lights from just that angle in the backseat of a different car so many years before? Who knows? Memory is not a recording device; sometimes it's a reckoning.

I've been capable of discussing my incest experience as a function of my culture's failings for decades now. But details, stories that would seem like fiction if they hadn't happened, can still emerge.

At first, in that taxi years later, I didn't remember who I was with while I was watching that reel-to-reel film. I know I saw the beginning of that film, back in the late seventies, in one of the casinos. How old was I? Which boyfriend was that? Why on earth were we in Las Vegas?

Oh, right, I was there with my mother, while she was dating the man she'd marry. Had she married him yet at that moment? Had he begun using me as his implement of pleasure, of shame, of devotion, of respite, of release? Had I yet become his courtesan, his tramp, his comedian, his conversationalist, his squaw, his half-breed, his Lolita, his stop-looking-at-me-like-that-you-just-don't-understand-the-way-the-world-is? Was that snuff film before or after I was already...

It doesn't matter when it was. It was just a curiosity, something he wanted to see, something he thought might shock me. Or maybe prepare me. I don't know what he meant by taking me in there after my mother went up to bed. I didn't stay until the end. I stood up with the film still moving on the screen, the woman being fucked and roughed up a bit. Her mounting fear was in the back of my throat. I walked back out into the casino and got lost because I could smell danger. The room on screen looked like my room in that very hotel. I think it was the Imperial Palace Hotel. Could that be right? It's not called that anymore. The building has been sold and resold, remodeled and refurbished—a postmodern form of erasure. A shiny, new version stands in its place, as though it never existed.

A lot of people are talking about it these days: how can all these women come forward years after an assault and speak up now? This is a story about how we come to remember and become capable of holding the memory, rather than pushing it away. Often, one is less imperiled when the memory holds rather than slipping swiftly under the sea of consciousness. Is it possible for a woman to be un-imperiled, fully safe? I don't think so. This is the story you need to hear, and because it's printed in ink, on paper, you can come back to it later, even if you can't hold all of it now.

How did I remember? Slowly. I walked into the casino with confidence and an assured upright survival that people say I was born with. Well, I must've gotten it somewhere. That's what people said but often in moments when it sounded like they needed an excuse.

II.

I remember attending another conference, twenty-some years ago, not in Las Vegas. (This is a scene in the same drama. You won't be able to see that at first, but it is. It will seem so different because I am no longer a child, and hotels can contain varied activities, and Las Vegas casinos are a little bit sleazy anyway. It will seem as though nothing is the same, but these stories are related.)

I was doing a speaking engagement about incest and activism for a group of therapists, social workers, and psychiatrists. I had been invited to talk about incest and child sexual abuse as an outgrowth of sexism. I was representing a grassroots organization of survivor-activists I had cofounded in order to do community education and build survivor solidarity. My intention was to help this group to discuss how our broader cultural values undergird subtle acceptance of violence and the sexualization of children. I intended to discuss our interconnectedness, though we worked from different perspectives, experiences, and training on this topic. I wanted to raise awareness about the social patterning in the prevalence of rape and incest and violence against children.

After years of peer support and training in sociology, my own understanding had shifted from seeing myself as an incest survivor, to saying that I was raised in an incest family, to discussing all of the ways that we each live in an incest-supporting culture. All of us. A sociological view on this topic might well help us make something new, I believed. I specifically positioned myself as an expert, based on my experiences—not just my training. To my mind, this was an important aspect of my credibility on the topic.

Those mental health professionals didn't see me as a colleague. They saw me as an articulate client. An articulate patient. An angry, fucked-up woman with a wound I tried to justify sharing but could never escape. For them, I was an aftermath, and breaking into the explosion site to do a little poking through the rubble was going to be the only interesting or useful way to interact with me. I could act like a colleague, and if I kept myself from mentioning all of this personal experience with the topic, they would grudgingly treat me like one, but that's not the path I chose to take. And so there I was, talking about damage as though it was a site of wisdom, and to them that was nonsense. Just nonsense. It can't be justified, not with education or language and certainly not by showing up at this meeting in my overly voluptuous "so, did you ever do prostitution?" body.

That was the first inappropriate question.

And then, "So, say something more about your self-harm patterns."

At that time in my life, I thought sharing my own story, for the greater good, meant that I should answer every question asked. I wasn't born answering every question asked, but I learned it. Sometimes it seemed like too much effort to resist answering. They were simply the wrong questions. I answered questions about drugs and eating disorders and recovery. I wanted to get back to my point about the "incest culture," but, yeah, whatever. Answer the question asked. Now I know better. I was younger then.

They kept talking about recovery. My recovery. Not the culture's recovery. The impossibility of recovery. What did that mean to them? "Recovery."

At that conference, more than twenty years ago, a man stood up and told me that I *would never fully recover*. Or if I had—I mean, if I truly was what I purported to be: a fully functioning adult capable of forming relationships and having a family—then I was some kind of miracle and maybe I could enlighten the group about my so-called "recovery." I mean, psych wards are full of women who'd endured the same experiences I stood calmly describing, so, you know, who the hell did I think I was?

Was he fucking nuts? That's what I thought back then. I mean, who's entitled to call someone crazy? It sure wasn't me. Some small part of my mind has been working on how to answer him all this time since.

I couldn't find the right words, but eventually I'd definitely had enough. I mean, well and truly enough, and I left that room, in the same way I'd left the snuff film, calmly, like I was just going out to the restroom, would return with my lipstick freshened. I left, looking down at my blue-and-white spectator pumps on my stockinged feet, clicking out of the room in my corporate drag, upright and confident, not sure what to say, but sure enough that he was an asshole who had no idea how to ask the right questions if his life depended on it. Fucking psychologists!

I'm not the type who would say that terrible experiences are there to teach us something. I wouldn't say that, though they sure set you up to learn something if you can manage to learn it. I am still addressing that asshole psychologist, psychiatrist, or whatever he was, along with every disrespectful person like him when I write and talk about the culture we collectively create. I learned something that day about the credibility others allow me to have and how it runs up against the credibility I have earned inside of myself, and in community with others who know that we are neither ignorant nor powerless. I learned how not to accept a diminished place, though one is given to me over and over again. I learned from those before me who remained undiminished by circumstances, and from my own ability to move out of harm's way in one setting after another. I am still learning and have it in me to learn and teach.

How would your life be different if you could change the way you think about belonging? Rather than saying "I don't belong here," you could say "they don't accommodate me here." How would that help you find others with whom you could make positive change?

I am "recovered" in the same way that a tree that grows around the obstacle of a fence or an electrical line is "recovered." That is to say, it was never broken. It simply grew around that which it could not move. And I am damaged in the same way that we are all damaged when something spoils the water supply and poison sinks into the roots of every tree in the forest, every small plant and every creature drinking at the water source. Poison alters every bit of soil for a long time to come. I am both damaged and recovered and undamaged and able to teach and show you something, doctor, because I care enough about others to be standing here opening my mouth.

You may see nothing but a disaster site, and my life is the aftermath, but I am asking you to look more closely. I am the whole landscape, not just the rubble. I am still speaking to you, doctor, because I understand that the views you felt so entitled to express in public are still in the unconscious hearts of many. We need to keep working with ourselves and each other, even when we'd rather check out and let someone else handle it.

And, doctor, though you think you know all about women like me, I know better than to let you frame all the questions. Some people take credibility for granted. Others wait their turn, even if it never comes. People like me know that we need to find creative ways to lay claim to the ground we were given at birth, to be contributors to the culture that holds us all.

I am speaking to you, doctor. Are you listening? You know victims—and you think you know them well. Does that mean you know perpetrators too? You probably know them better than you admit. Here is what I meant to say to you in that room twenty years ago: "Sit down and stop talking for a little while, especially in that nasty tone. I am here to teach you, sir, not to be your specimen."

It's possible to listen better, to see more, even when—like that doctor—it was not our original training. You can see the way men and women look at each other at work and on dates and in porno films and TV shows, and all the little bombs waiting to go off just become part of the scenery. No one need speak of them aloud. Every landscape is like one of those children's magazine puzzles. The instruction says, "Find forty bombs in this picture." And at first you don't see any. Then you do. And there's another and you're on a roll, so there's one and there's one and there's one. Of course, turn the image on its side; there's one over here too.

III.

How do your memories come through?

Can you remember what shoes you were wearing when you first felt that you were better than another human being? Or does a scent bring back the feeling of arousal when you know you're going to get what you want? Maybe it's the feel of your sweater sleeves under your fingertips that lets you recall your own abuse or how your privileges will let you hurt others later. If you have ever looked away from something painful—I think all of us have—how do you sit quietly through the feelings of danger you must surely feel at times?

Now, how do you come to question what you were taught? What obstacles did you grow around, or did the poison you drank from our common water source become a cherished part of your daily sustenance?

How do you make sense—now, as an adult—of the first pornography you ever saw? How old were you? Where did you see it and what did you feel in your body?

You may wonder how this question is relevant to the discussion of incest culture and social change. We are talking about the terrible things that happened to me as a result of that snuff film, aren't we? But not even really as a result, because there was no cause and effect circumstance that could bring indictment. This isn't relevant, you say, but look closely at the image where you've been asked to find forty bombs. Turn the page to the side, then upside down. Turn it clockwise and then counterclockwise. All of these stories belong in the same book where we learn to see what we cannot see. These stories hang together in the same web of slender, powerful strands that connect one thing to another. This is still the same story.

When you were eleven—the age at which most men started watching pornography of their own volition—what did you learn about sex and how did you make sense of it? If you saw pornography, were there images of people having sex *with* each other, or of women enjoying subjugation? How did you make sense of what you saw, in the context of your everyday life? If you were a boy, somehow you knew that girls your age did not seem like they would enjoy watching such things. You don't assume they watch such things, and, for the most part, you're right. If you were a girl who was interested in sex, chances are you got very different messages about your interests than boys did. Even if no one called you a slut, you knew that would be the name for you if you spoke too much about it. Children are often taught that men and women are just different, or that boys and girls are different—or maybe that adults are just different from children. The messages about how sex can be something other than lust or duty are out there—but like crackling on a radio. No clear information comes through. If you didn't consider other possibilities then, might you consider them now and add nuance to that memory of your first pornography and how it felt in your body?

People of all genders can enjoy sexual dominance, sexual submission, and a wide range of other innovative sexual practices, so why would I bother gendering this conversation at all? Patterns illuminate what we've hidden from ourselves. They are like the hints at the back of the magazine where each bomb is outlined in dark ink. And while an interest in sex and the ability to innovate sexually and handle erotic power are the domain of all people, there are clear patterns in how dominance and submission in media follow pre-established lines of oppression in our culture. Humans are both creating and consuming media, and, while overt sexism and racism (which include humiliation and name-calling) have been removed from most popular media, they have not been removed from pornographic media. All people are capable of sexuality, and most have erotic urges. Deviations are interesting, of course, and often the larger patterns go unexamined.

How do you make sense of what you see on the screen when you watch pornography now? Do you think about it at all, or is it just normal that "sex for pay" is so stylized? It is styled for its main consumers: men and boys. How do you understand yourself as a consumer? How do you think you can tell the difference between consent and slavery and coercion born of circumstance beyond one's control?

The most important question for all of us in a consumer culture:

how do we understand the difference between sex and what sex-as-industry has become?

Pornography is a multi-billion dollar industry and one we rarely discuss openly, in the same ways we discuss fair wages and worker treatment at Walmart, McDonald's, and Amazon. If we don't start considering how to create systems that draw distinctions about agency and give women control over their own sexuality and livelihoods, then we are absolutely encouraging slavery—and, in an industry where youth is prized, we're encouraging child sexual abuse as well. People who are regular consumers need to place themselves as such, rather than remaining the naughty children who watched that porn the first time, the first ten times, for the first ten years.

I worry that we're losing the erotic wisdom that could be prompting acceptance of diverse bodies, greater pleasure, understanding, and love. I'm in favor of sex and creativity and erotic brilliance. Consenting humans are magnificent, and they should use all media they can conceive to amplify and share their fortune.

I am concerned about pornography as industry, the business of it, the hierarchy in it, the patterns that inspire desire in a misogynist child-using culture. How do you get so close to a blast site without getting hurt? How do you do it, again and again, light the fuse and run. Do we even know how well we've learned to plant the bombs?

Snuff films in the 1970s may well have been a sales-stunt, not involving actual death. Still, an audience emerged and another audience on the fringe of the first who wouldn't say they wanted to fuck and murder someone but would watch it nonetheless. For curiosity's sake. For shock. For fun. Like my stepfather.

And now, decades on, it's normal to see women choked and humiliated, eyes bulging—just normal in pornography—funny to some—and normal. Of course choking and humiliation are erotic expression for some women. But most women? How many eleven year-old girls? What is normal? Who is on the receiving end of *normal*?

I think these are good questions. I don't want a society of obedient boys who wish they were watching porn but abstain from it for the sake of decorum. I want a society of men who have come to understand their sexual urges as part of their vast humanity and who simply cannot be turned on by another's victimization. I want processes by which we seek to know the difference between sex and oppression.

Submission without oppression.

Dominance without oppression.

These are possible.

Look who's asking the questions now, doctor. You are implicated in this culture we create, and so am I. Every person we meet, every message and image we consume, has helped to create us, and this is good news because we are culture-makers too. We are capable of creating culture that honors human expression rather than casting some people in narrow roles with no exits.

How do we recover from what my incest family and our incest-supporting culture did to me? What of the people you know and love who never told you about being abused because they couldn't bear the burden of your listening? How can we listen now? Did you look at the woman on the screen being fucked and interpret sounds of pleasure or sounds of her choking or images of her receiving treatment that you know, I mean you know, must hurt or damage or kill? Did you believe it when she stood up afterward and acted like everything was good? I mean, she laughed after she did that disgusting humiliating thing. Surely that means she's in on the joke. Surely she got paid. This is what you tell yourself.

How can we make space for those who say "this is not good"? How can we hear them and make sure the world holds them too?

Work for pay is often still different for men, women, and other-gendered people. No act of desire is unfettered by economic consequences in a world where pornography is an industry. How do you love and get turned on and fuck and honor and feel and live? We can choose what's sold as sex in our mutual culture.

One of the most common responses young men have nowadays to watching images of sexual humiliation is that "it's hilarious." Peggy Orenstein found this in her research for the book *Girls and Sex*. Those boys are spectators, being entertained; they usually feel no empathy. They think they can construct distance through language and collusion. They think they have distance, but I think they are mistaken. Might they remember those girls being humiliated, years from now, once we've engaged a deeper erotic wisdom and everyone's pleasure matters? I hope they remember and weep as they look down at their shoes, their hands, up at their surroundings, and know that they were hurt by cultural expectations too.

None of us are undamaged, but some of us learned to survive, then thrive and celebrate being alive in whatever amazing shapes our lives have taken. All of us have formed ourselves around the obstacles we found as we grew. It's just that some of us can name those obstacles and others remain ignorant. They think themselves fully formed and perfect in their perceptions. Not damaged, like me.

2.

BODIES IN MOTION

That little blue bicycle with the banana seat was an extension of my body and soul. I rode around the big empty hospital office building early in the morning, hands never on the handlebars. I'd work up speed and then take my feet from the pedals, waving my arms, circus-style, switching to sidesaddle or putting my feet up on the handlebars for kicks. I never wiped out. No pain, no scabs, no scars. Never. I once spent a quarter in one of those machines where a mystery gift pops out in a plastic bubble. It turned out to be a sticker with a funny little blue faerie-devil on it and the words "Blue Imp." I stuck it on the front of my bicycle at the helm. I was in fourth grade—eight years old. I rode around as often as I could, no friends around the apartment where we lived, waiting for our house to be remodeled. My father left us during that remodel, so it was a long wait. My sugar cravings were already in full bloom, fueled by my mother's disgust at watching me eat it, and at me being fat. She'd reluctantly buy me a milkshake with my burger at the fast food joints where we often dined and say, "It's like poison." Or "I wish you wouldn't eat that." Sometimes I rode my bike down to the donut shop, farther than I was actually allowed to go on the big busy street. I'd buy however many donuts I could with change I found around the house. I wasn't afraid of that street. I was nimble on the Blue Imp, not too heavy at all.

Today, I am watching kids, probably eight to fifteen years old, playing on a pier. Two of them have climbed up onto a large broken metal and wood structure; perhaps it had been a small billboard. Their parents would probably yell for them to come down, if they were looking. Eight boys and two girls, shoving each other and playing. The two boys up on the structure look down and jeer, daring.

The older girl—maybe fourteen—makes for the structure. She is a formidable climber in her white shorts and halter top. Her lean brown body seems unconcerned with decorum and appearances. I marvel at her physical problem-solving. When she approaches, the two boys are already high atop the wooden whatsit; she sets about figuring out how to climb it. They laugh at her failed attempts, and then she figures it out. Part climbing, part jumping from pole to structure. She stands tall and triumphant—the trio some twenty feet above the pier. Sixty feet at least above the water below. The other kids look on impressed as they joke and push at each other, standing on the solid wooden planks.

I am watching from a rented kayak, bobbing in the water near the shore. I am also impressed by the girl on the high-up structure—because of the climbing and because she's a girl. She has more to overcome on that climb than the boys, so it's all the more courageous that she does it. It'd be easy to say that she's just overcoming stereotypes and those are mental, so climb away! But stereotypes and expectations are carried in the body. They become ability or failure in the eyes of others unevenly. She clearly has moxie and the tenacity to try and try again through the jeers.

By the time I was her age, I was more timid than the smaller girl who stands on the pier at a distance from the climbing triumph. I no longer rode a bike, found the world strangely cruel and beautiful and my body—well, I hadn't rejected it as some girls had, but I lived cautiously, having embraced the story that a fat body was rather weak and socially useless. In private, intimate moments, I knew my body was a miracle. Looking up from my kayak, bobbing gently in the sea, I recall the joy of a trustworthy body and how I would rediscover my own athleticism in my twenties and thirties then lose it again in my late forties.

Over fifty now, the feeling of the kayak being an extension of my body—as the Blue Imp was—eludes me. I stay close to shore and enjoy the bob and sway as others head to deeper waters. I feel shaky and scared when confronted by swells or chop, and I fear falling out and not being able to get back in, my body a spectacle as I struggle. The boat *is* an extension of my body, of course, so the more I wobble in fear, the more the boat threatens to tip. I work to level my breathing. Relax my shoulders, enjoy and stretch my current abilities. I remind myself that this body deserves my constant reclamation from the social sea that would sooner see it drowned.

As I watch the young woman in shorts and halter top, her slim body trying to ascend, turning back, ascending again, her body awkwardly wedged and then free in her repeated attempts, I realize that much of the decorum bodies like mine feel is the result of stigma management. Sure, she looks more awkward than ladylike, her butt sticking out at times, her arms quivering with effort; her sweaty, capable movements carry their own social stigma related to femininity. But my body is a spectacle even when I am sitting still, and stillness, full containment of movement, is the only thing that diminishes public ridicule.

It's a cruel setup, the way thin people cajole us toward exercise, to lose weight, for our own good. The fat body in movement is a travesty—even when amazingly powerful. Fat female weightlifters, shot-putters, discus throwers are derided for the way their fat arms protrude from T-shirt sleeves. The way the belly becomes visible in a moment of twisting is considered reprehensible.

I am keenly aware that one might say to a thin girl: "Pull down your shirt; it's riding up." Whereas one would say to a fat girl: "Pull down your shirt; your belly is showing." Both are body-policing commentary yet very different in intent. The first statement speaks to the shame of revealing the female body, the dangers of potential assault that girls are made to carry. The second speaks of the shame of revealment plus. The shame of ugliness plus. The second statement contains the first, along with the shame of being wrong-bodied and likely deserving manifold abuses. If such a body were to be assaulted, specifically sexually assaulted, the body whose belly is deemed un-see-able should also feel a bit grateful for the attention.

Pull your shirt down. It's riding up.

Pull your shirt down. Your belly is showing.

Clothing necessarily moves around the body in movement. When the body is in motion, exerting itself, engaged in physical problem-solving, it becomes visible. The difference between the shirt riding up and the belly showing can be the difference between acceptance and ridicule, life and death.

It would be easy to say that I accomplished physical fitness in my youth by "not caring" what other people were thinking of my body. In part, it's true. I had to come into the experience of my body, rather than focusing on the appearance of my body in order to go all-in at the gym, in the dance class, in the yoga studio. And, at the same time, I was always aware of my body's appearance. How could I not be, in such a world? Physical mastery of every task was needed in order to keep me showing up. Otherwise, the burden of insults and pity would have simply been too great. In my youth, when people opened their mouths to speak about my body, it was to say I was graceful (for a fat woman) or strong (for a fat woman). Sure, the parenthetical was always there, but being impressive comes first. That's stigma management. While wearing exercise clothes was itself radical, I was in constant relationship with my clothes, choosing what to show and what to conceal. Some days still, my ability to bare my upper arms in a yoga class, for instance, is a challenge. The ability to bare my belly publicly, most days, is still beyond me.

Some fat women never risk movement at all because of shame and fear of ridicule. There is logic in this choice. Tragic (and often invisible) logic.

What I see in the girl's body, high above the water, is pleasure and triumph. I remember the way breeze feels on skin on a hot day. I am grateful for what her joy teaches me, and for the movement of the sea beneath me as I watch her. I am fearful and floating and losing my calm and finding it again and enjoying my small triumph of being in a kayak at all. This is an act of reclamation. The last time, ten years ago, I was with a group and became too fearful to keep up in choppy water. I turned back to shore and felt failure, not pleasure. Today, I am afraid and grateful, and the sun is shining; everything glistens.

Just yesterday, at this very beach, I took up a conversation with a fat woman on the shore. She was sitting in the sand, with the water lapping up over her legs as I ambled into the water. Of course I noticed her, the bikini in particular, because she was a fat woman, about my size, and I quite enjoy noting how many young fat women are now wearing bikinis at the beach.

Once in the water, I floated easily, then paddled about. I could feel her watching me as I dug my feet into the soft sand, picked up shells and examined them as I jounced along. One of us struck up a conversation about the beauty of the shore or the weather—who knows; we were both affable conversationalists. She said she was afraid of the water and that, though she was staying by the shore for the summer, she never went in. She was from Wisconsin. I marveled at her bathing suit and travel bravery—alone on a summer-long adventure, juxtaposed against her swimming timidity. She hadn't been in the water once.

I grew up in fear. I was probably nine years old when I realized that I was likely the weight of an adult woman. In any case, I wasn't the size of a child, so I became aware that most "child things" were not for me. Always admonished for not exercising more, always insulted in movement, this is how we grow. At SeaWorld, during a school trip, I self-consciously noted that the weight limit on one of the playable attractions was 110 pounds. I already weighed near 130. I imagined the attraction tearing apart under the weight of my body. I imagined falling through it or, worse yet, being the reason that other children fell through it. I imagined ridicule. Sometimes, I imagined that something would go terribly wrong as a result of my body and I wouldn't even deserve to be rescued. I'd actually die, with others laughing at me in pity and disgust.

The young woman watched me for quite a while in the nearly currentless water. And then she said, "It looks so lovely. Maybe I won't be swept out." I imagined her imaginings—her lifeless body being pulled to shore and dragged, no further poise in her flesh, onlookers laughing. I saw the way she looked at the sea, worried, and I imagined her fear, smiled, and invited her in.

Soon, she was floating beside me. Though it wasn't likely that any ill would befall us, there in the soothing sea, fear and anticipatory shame can so easily excise us from the company of others, leave us without love and care. How much easier was it for that young woman to have another fat lady around, I pondered? Or maybe, I simply understood, how much easier it would've been for the younger aspect of myself— always calculating the possibility of disaster with no one like me doing the bold thing, the daring thing. There was hardly ever anyone like me doing anything physical at all. Comrades remind us how pleasure and triumph look in bodies like our own.

When the choice comes to let the fat body be seen in struggle or be still, most will choose stillness.

The girl in the white halter top and shorts breathes heavily for a few moments high above the pier, arms akimbo, feet planted firmly, resting after her ascent. She is my role model for today; she has reminded me of my relationship with the Blue Imp. She and the two boys start to wrestle then, each trying to knock the others off the platform into the water. She identifies with them and their laughing cries make them kindred. Somehow, we are all connected for just a moment, in body pleasure, water-air-sun-sea pleasure. We are earthbound human-community-creating animals. I am bobbing along in my kayak, wobbling with the fear that was inscribed upon my body long ago. I am staying with myself, my own breath, aware that my too-small life jacket draws attention to my body. I am breathing and smiling and squinting up at them. I am not letting my belly show, as I watch her joyful scuffle and the way her shirt rides up again as they all fall-jump at once, push apart, each body separate, limbs stretched like stars midair, contracting into spears as they pierce the glistening water.

3.

I SAID "NO" IN THREE LANGUAGES

East Flanders is laced with lovely paths for biking and walking. Through farms and along the canals they connect tiny towns and larger roadways. Sometimes I am alone on the path, flanked only by cows and goats, sheep and geese. On Sunday afternoons, the bike and foot traffic is persistent. One Wednesday afternoon, I walked silently, noticing the slight greening of a field that was turned just a few days back. Geese flew up from the canal as a barge went by. And then a man on a bicycle approached from behind and slowed to speak to me. I smiled, shook my head, and told him in English that I didn't speak Flemish.

In an instant, I knew it. He wasn't pausing to ask directions or tell me something about the town or bridge ahead or that I'd dropped my notebook from my bag. He was giving me the look, chin jutting slightly, eyes taking in too much of me, considering I didn't know him. If these looks, comments, stops, and demands for attention weren't so persistent across time and geography, it might be possible to argue that the poor guy meant nothing by it. I imagined the ill intent. But does every woman imagine the leers, the tone of voice? No. We could write books, compose symphonies, paint masterpieces showing the nuances and persistence of men's subjugating behavior toward all who are not men.

I am nearly fifty years old. How many times in my life has this scene occurred? No way to count, because we learn early to dismiss these moments as part of the landscape, nothing worth noting, but for noting silently what we are wearing, who is around, how we could've put ourselves in danger and what we might've done or been to invoke such attention. These are the moments when the mind reviews that familiar landscape of self-blame. The body tightens slightly, ready for the kind of intrusion, maybe harm, which feels inevitable, if not deserved.

This is how the story goes, a foreign film without subtitles, yet meaning remains clear.

He spoke to me, and I smiled, nodded. And then he spoke again, riding slow, just ahead of my walking, then crossing back and forth ahead of me to slow his ride, but also to block my path. I kept my pace and smiled. Then his face grew irritated at my lack of verbal response. Middle-aged white man, bad teeth, wearing farmer's clothes. These details made him merely Flemish on a country road, no more. He could've been a man of any appearance. And so I spoke, to re-route his irritation. I said I don't speak Flemish, and perhaps he asked me where I was from. I said that I spoke English and German, smiled, and shrugged at his further talking. Perhaps to him this seemed that I was inviting conversation in one of those languages, which I really didn't mean to do, but this was a bind. No way to avoid hostility without seeming to invite something. *More.*

He spoke again; he slowed and seemed to ask me to slow down too, but I did not. And maybe he was speaking German but with such a strong accent I couldn't understand. Or maybe my mind could not multitask the understanding of an accented foreign language with the other task it had just been given—it's that thing we do—of assessing the surroundings. Instead of seeing greening fields, fluffy sheep, I considered the landscape for exits (field, canal, path), for human company (none visible in either direction, perhaps a kilometer all around), for his stature (could I take him? I'm big but never sure, especially as I age).

He was speaking still, and louder, coaxing me to stop and move off the path with him. He rolled ahead and motioned again for me to stop, which I did not. Still smiling, I gestured toward the town as destination, never slowed down. He rode on beside me, and there it was. I saw the turning moment, as I have so often before, where my management of our interaction was vital: his irritation, small twitch, set jaw. He reasserted his desire that I stop my transit, and, though I'd been shaking my head already, I added the words in English, then in German, and as I was speaking, firmly through my smile, I thought to add in French as well. "J'ai dit que non." I had said no. In three languages now I said it. Still smiling, walking, looking toward the town ahead which could not be seen, but best we both imagine it. He rode beside me, spoke some more, and then, disgusted, shook his head, gestured me off, and rode away.

• • •

A few years ago, I was invited to offer storytelling as a keynote for an "obesity research" conference in Canada. My storytelling performances about bodies in culture—gender, race, sexuality, size—are invited at conferences as a way to explore a theme in a different format, as a way to connect participants' thinking and feeling selves. The invitation itself was not unusual, but the audience was. So when I had the organizer on the phone, I said, "Thanks so much for inviting me. But I'm curious. How did the committee choose *me*? I'm not usually invited to events that use the term 'obesity.' I find that language pathologizing to fat bodies. Usually my views aren't welcome at conferences like this."

I prefer to use "fat" as a neutral descriptive adjective (in defiance of its cultural non-neutrality), much as one might use blonde, tall, or D/ deaf to describe a person. Though I expressed curiosity about my inclusion, I was indeed pleased to reach a group of people who'd likely never considered my views and perspective before.

The organizer confirmed that, indeed, not everyone was happy to have me as keynote, but that a small group of qualitative researchers on the organizing committee felt it was important to include me. A few of the medical professionals already intended to boycott my presentation. The organizer said part of the reason they invited me in particular was that they wanted to gently persuade their colleagues that they should care about fat stigma. They should care about the perspectives of the people with whom they work.

"I don't know how to say this," she said, "but, you're … nice. You're likeable." I nodded as she spoke, understanding immediately. Her committee found my themes valuable, my analysis solid, and, still, I am funny, entertaining, and know how to handle an audience. Nice.

Being nice is a performative choice. There's an art to smiling and subtly engaging bullies without agreeing with them. (Though there's always a danger that kindness will be read as capitulation.) Being nice doesn't mean I'm not angry or frightened or sad or anxious. It means I'm calling upon a demeanor that works in a certain situation. It can be an unconscious response, no doubt a habituated response to specific people or stimuli. Some women, once they shake off the learned response of niceness toward bullies can't reclaim it again as choice. Fair enough. Yet I am not unconscious, for the most part; being nice is a choice, which does not mean it is an act. Niceness is not merely gendered weakness. Niceness is complex.

• • •

As I was walking recently in downtown Hilo, Hawaii, two brown-skinned men—probably in their thirties, perhaps part Polynesian—stopped in the street to comically "appreciate" me. They didn't try to lure me off the path, yet they were in my way, performing flattery to bring me pleasure and cause me to appreciate them in return. Their words and actions seemed more an act of bonding between the two of them than a way to manipulate my behavior beyond simple sociability. One leapt dramatically in front of me, legs spread, arms wide and said, "Eh tutu!" while leering at me, head dramatically moving up and down to take in my body. His friend smiled and joined him, saying, "You looking good, ma'am," similarly leering. I shook my head and chuckled, walking past. The humor in that encounter came in part from their language choice, acknowledging that I was older than they. And their clowning was silly, midday, in a well-populated area.

Have you wondered yet what I was wearing in either of these street harassment examples? How I looked? More clues are coming. And note that you will already have an opinion on what each clue means. One more example, though, to show that I do not perform only "niceness." I offer irritation and correction too.

The farmer's market is less than half a mile from my home. Though this is my story, different versions of it play out regularly. They're happening now to someone; they will keep happening all day, around the world, and they will happen again tomorrow.

As I leave the market on foot with my bag of vegetables, a man, perhaps in his late twenties, walks next to me, a few feet away. He seems stoned. He's giving me "the look" and keeping pace with me. He begins talking, mumbling, gesturing with his chin toward my body and my face as he speaks. It goes something like this: "Mumble mumble, hot sexy, mumble, slurp, like to get a taste, mumble, mumble, slurp."

I pause and say, "Excuse me? I can't hear what you're saying. Are you trying to speak to me?" He nods and leers and walks beside me, yet apart, from the parking lot to the road, and one more time he says, "Mumble mumble, want to let me, slurp, mumble" and he gestures toward his car, opens his arms and smiles to indicate my bountiful size and tastiness. He punctuates with a lewd pelvic twitch. I put up a hand and say, "No. And if you have something to say to someone, speak up and say it."

I am irritated to be waylaid, wearing sandals and a sundress, uncombed hair, previously unconscious of my appearance as I quickly left the house. And even now, I'd rather be thinking about what I'm making for lunch. I'm not working today, and I don't want to be nice. Wanting to be left alone has come to feel selfish. This is not nothing. I have taken a day off from managing this behavior, but he has not taken a day off from pursuit. I feel pressed into service and the beets bound for juicing are heavy in my bag. Then his car is beside me, riding slow. He persists, mumbling and slurping like a hungry fool. I say, "Please go away." And he leaves but circles around and back again. I am about a block from my home.

I think, oh, hell no, you're not following me all the way to my house! We are in my neighborhood, surrounded by people I know within shouting distance. Or is it perhaps the absurdity of his age and approach that raises my ire? I perceive him as a child who requires correction, and so I stop, irritated and parental, to speak to him through the open passenger-side window. A few feet from the car, speaking loudly enough for him to hear me clearly, I say, "Okay, look. What you're doing here is creepy. You're actually following me home, and I'm not having that. I am on foot, and you're following me in a car. Creepy! If you want to ask someone for sex, ask someone who seems like they want sex, not someone who's out grocery shopping. Ask in a tone of voice and volume that can be heard. And if a person's not interested in your advances, then GO AWAY."

I am in full oratory now, and he's still leering and gesturing with his chin and then slowly he begins to look more at his lap. "And look," I say, "someone needs to tell you this because, I don't know why! Maybe you're too young to know better and I am old enough to be your mother. In fact, who is your mother? Do you live around here? Does your family live near here? We live in a small community here, and what you're doing is creepy!"

To which he says, chin on chest, "I'm sorry, ma'am." And drives away. I call after his car, "That's better!" and carry my groceries home.

• • •

In my youth, before I knew better, I accepted my mother's admonitions that I dressed too provocatively. I accepted friends' and teachers' assessments that I was cultivating an outlandish look that would draw weirdos. As a teenager, I'd shake my head and say, "Yeah, I'm a weirdo magnet. Maybe it's because of how I look."

The term "weirdos" may be appropriate to describe the men who feel the need to gawk and talk and threaten and compliment and proposition and divert my time and energy. It's weird, though common. But this language conceals important things: gender, habituated gendered behavior, male bonding rituals, gender socialization. It's not that I attract weirdos. It's not even that I attract men. It's that often—really often—men feel entitled to objectify, belittle, harass, talk to, flirt with, proposition, and bully any women they choose.

I have on occasion attracted mere weirdos. I was once sitting in a café, writing in a notebook, bare feet up on a chair, flowing clothes and multi-colored hair falling around me. A woman walked up and said, "I saw you when I walked in. I'm a witch and you're a vibrant, sensual being with an important message for humanity." I looked up at her and thought to myself, now, you're a weirdo and maybe the way I look attracted you. I said, "Aha. Okay. Thanks. So, I'm sitting here doing some quiet writing. I'm not really interested in conversation, but if you want to pull up a chair, you can share the table." And she did. We did our own things. When I stood to leave, we exchanged names and pleasantries, and she said a few more freaky things. That's what an exchange with a weirdo looks like.

But the way men treat me when they choose to engage in street harassment—that has nothing to do with me.

"What you're talking about doesn't happen to all women." My girlfriend said this one day as I rehearsed a story for a reading about street harassment. She's a bit older than I am and could only recall a handful of men who'd ever catcalled her. Her whole life. She said she liked it. It made her feel like part of a group of women to which she didn't always feel she belonged.

I looked her up and down, trying to put on "the male gaze."

"You're scary," I concluded. She's 6'2. She wears men's clothes and if she's in a bad humor, or simply walking alone, she looks like she could kick your ass and not be sorry. I love some of those things about her. She doesn't always read like she's a woman or a target. She doesn't always receive "the behavior." Her demeanor deflects the entitlement many men feel.

Me, I don't fight. I don't run. I've never been fast or extra-strong, and, just like my girlfriend, I sometimes enjoyed street harassment as a young person because my culture taught me that fat girls would never get love. Something about street harassment feels like the precursor to love: attention. If you're invisible, how will you ever get love?

This is what we manage, along with social expectations, on the street. How can I keep the attention I think I need and direct it, not get hurt, not be used? It's up to me to attract it and deflect it and incite men to be wonderfully wild yet prevent them from being savage. I am the conductor for an entire cultural orchestra of gendered behavior. That's what I learned. Even at age eleven, when my body turned from child to fireworks, I was supposed to be an expert conductor of male behavior. That's what we all learned.

If you're invisible, how will you ever get … anything? Just as fat girls are taught to be grateful for any attention we get, all women are taught that rallying male attention is important to basic survival. This is not an overt lesson, but the message is ubiquitous nonetheless. So we cultivate the "right" kinds of visibility. Men and women live separate lives, after all. Sure, we often live in the same houses, always in the same towns. We make and parent children, and most of us came from two-gender households.

Yet many men and women still find cross-gender friendships odd. And traditionally (which means even today), when women are going about their own business, they're working in jobs, raising children, cooking meals, cleaning, socializing (primarily with other women), teaching, making things, and so on. Traditionally, when men are going about their own business, they're working in jobs, working in government, in medicine, in city infrastructure, in religion, socializing (primarily with other men), teaching, and watching or playing sports. We are not always involved in the same pursuits. And how dramatically do the impacts of our pursuits differ?

Even if these statements seem like generalizations for which exceptions are easily conjured, they are statistically true. Men still comprise less than 5 percent of workers in fields like secretarial work and child care, and women represent less than 5 percent of airline pilots and firefighters. And politics? Just look at a photo of Congress members—or any group of elected officials. Our eyes are trained to focus on anomalies—the three or four red skirt-suits among the sea of men's blue suits. We'd like to think equity is near, when it is not. The orchestration of male attention—often, male permission—is not incidental to women's lives. Not on the street, not anywhere.

My choice to be nice is not merely an act. I choose it sometimes to enhance my chances of safety. But more often—on stage, as a teacher, in my public life, and in my community—I choose it because I understand that many people behave poorly out of habit. Otherwise thoughtful people turn dastardly because they've learned role-specific behavior; it's expected. They don't know how else to forge relationships, handle urges, manage friendships, deal with rejection and frustration, and it's painful to be corrected—especially by those whom they believe they should dominate. I'm referring to street harassment by men—directed at women and men. I'm referring to social bullying by women—directed at women and men.

Social science studies (and a vast number of women's experiences) have shown that men aren't as often attracted to women who are smarter than them, or even as smart, or who are even good at things they value. Misogyny is deep. These are not conscious choices. The architecture of our daily pursuits remains unconscious, until it's not.

It isn't just that I am expected to be nice and a little dull. I *want* to be nice, when it serves me, and when I can muster it genuinely, because we are all damaged by this cultural malaise, and diminishing these experiences doesn't help. Saying, "Well, it's not that big a deal" doesn't help. We must be clear in our reconstruction of culture, and, still, others deserve my compassion. I deserve my compassion. And yours, but I'm only in control of what I give and how I receive. As Lucille Clifton said, "What they call you is one thing. What you answer to is another."

• • •

When I finished my talk at the obesity researchers' conference, a few of the medical doctors (and fewer lab researchers) seemed stunned by my very existence. It was as if they'd never allowed for a fat woman to be interesting and complex, able to discuss matters of importance, able to enjoy her body, consciously name and combat stigma. After all, women, fat people, people of color—all who endure stigma—are supposed to remain silent about it. That's the value in teaching us to blame ourselves for being bullied. We don't speak up for fear of shame and potential ridicule.

It was as though I was an apparition, an anomaly, and so, with the entitlement you'd expect, one by one this handful of men (they were men) approached me to take a medical history. Well, that's what they do, isn't it? They asked me about whether I had diabetes, whether I had high cholesterol. In which BMI category did I reside? They looked me up and down—probably Obesity 3, would that be right? One man, after our talk regarding my health, used this language: "Wow, well, you're valid. I mean, I would judge you valid. You're a healthy person. Wow." Mind you, I was not speaking on anything related to medical care, nor had I once mentioned my health or lack thereof, but this seemed to be the only context in which he could render me legible. I was speaking on stigma, on how certain bodies are socially sanctioned and how you can't separate the effects of fat in the body from the effects of being fat in the culture. The latter causes pain, lack of opportunity, impedes credibility, and compromises health. He couldn't hear what I had said until he'd judged me physically "valid," and he was astonished to be able to make this pronouncement. He's not alone. Most people don't interact with others outside of their social stereotypes. That's why simple conversation and time getting to know one another is the most radical tool for humanizing others whom we don't know.

And how often does that happen, casually, between men and women who are not considering romantic involvement?

Standing in a conference hall, next to a table full of coffee and napkins, I responded to the doctor's questions with patience. I was at work. My body was public. He had something to learn, and I was on the job.

The problem is, all women's bodies are treated as public bodies. Men have something to learn about how to interact respectfully. Those who don't think they have something to learn should be actively teaching other men the error of their ways, and, if they're not, they still have something to learn about social responsibility.

I'm good at this job. I tap into a well of compassion for others; I'm nice; I turn a phrase that can open dialogue. Not everyone will do that, nor should they. Sometimes I need a day off, but still I choose this work. Those who don't choose it should be left to their own lives—and able to create lives that don't require male attention or permission. They need many days off from helping men understand that they are behaving poorly. And they certainly need safety and respect and the credibility of being humans with specific experiences and expertise about the world.

On a canal path in East Flanders, some guy felt entitled to order me to stop what I was doing, get off the path, and interact with him. Consider the vile absurdity of this. At what point would it ever be a good idea for a woman to stop with an unknown and overbearing man—especially one who didn't speak her language—and follow him off the path into the trees? There is nothing, but nothing, in this charming Flemish countryside to suggest "bad neighborhood" or troubled surroundings, and those who know the man who menaced me would likely call him friend or neighbor, a nice guy, a regular guy. That's just it. A regular guy.

We're all somewhere on the road. Either moving toward or away from systemic misogyny. No one is standing still. Through stories and movement and language and how we assert our human dignity, we create culture. I know which way I'm going on that road. And for anyone moving toward more conscious interactions, I'll do my best to offer kindness along the way.

4.

HOW TO BECOME A RACIST ANTI-RACISM EDUCATOR

Sometimes, on the street, I'll notice a stranger wearing a print with stripes, and I'll chuckle inside and think, *what a fashion faux pas.* Then I wonder if she's unaware, or perhaps she "knows better" and is resisting fashion standards. I definitely enjoy deliberate deviance, but it's hard to know. Or I'll see a man in a suit coat that doesn't fit well. The sleeve may fall below the thumb, or the hem rides a bit too low on the hip. I'll wonder if he knows the effect this may have on his income or employability. The suit itself is office-conforming clothing, but off the rack, not done quite right to fit the body. I think these things, even as I acknowledge the pleasure in choosing clothing specifically for nonconformity, in order to indulge my own creativity.

The rules of fashion were important to my mother; she felt empowered by her mastery. I saw her receive the rewards of dressing well. As a fat girl who learned to cover "figure flaws" it was perhaps all the more difficult for me to become a fat woman who is comfortable wearing colors, prints, and clothing styles I find fun but that I was taught would inspire pity, laughter, or dismissal in others. I know these responses really happen. I also know that through nonconformity I can help break down the daily biases and barriers that create systems of oppression. As Audre Lorde said about being queer: "Your silence will not protect you." I may indeed take some focus off my identity as a fat woman through careful clothing choices, but even with that approach I will never receive thin privilege. I may receive slightly less fat oppression, but I will lose an opportunity to disrupt ways of thinking that diminish my humanity. I'd rather disrupt that common, often unnoticed oppressive thinking. So I wear the color orange at times—a color I love and that I was taught was not truly compatible with any skin tone and should certainly not be worn by anyone larger than a size four. I wear what I like, even though my mother's script about fashion is still subtitling my thoughts. It sometimes influences my choices, and in many cases I have grown beyond those values, so her voice is but one of many—in my own mind and in the world.

When I was a child, I watched *The Jeffersons* on television. It ran from 1975–1985. It was a show about race and social class in America, in addition to being a goofy comedy about family and apartment-living mishaps. George Jefferson had been a character on *All in the Family*, a show known for comedy, good acting, and daring script-writing about social issues. We were used to seeing white families on television, and George Jefferson was Archie Bunker's Black neighbor. In the spin-off, he'd done well enough with his dry-cleaning business to own a chain of stores. He'd moved "uptown," away from the Bunker family. The show not only depicted Black upward mobility and the complexities of a Black family employing a Black maid; it was touted as only the second show on American television to depict a Black family. (I guess *Sanford and Son* was not considered a "real" family by white American standards.) I was not allowed to regularly watch *Good Times* and *Sanford and Son*, which preceded *The Jeffersons* slightly. Was it because those families were poor and at least our family had social class in common with the Jeffersons? People in my childhood world—which did not include Black people—talked about those shows.

Literally the first Black person I'd ever seen, as a child, was a boy in my kindergarten class, circa 1972. My family lived in an upper-middle-class white suburban neighborhood. That child stayed only a week because, despite his parents being able to afford my private school, other parents weren't ready for racial integration and their views won the day. As a small child, that's all I came to know. During many years of my childhood, it wasn't clear to me whether Black people were entitled to the types of experiences I took for granted and whether, even if they had the money, they should be able to buy the things my family enjoyed. I knew for certain, from what I'd been told in my first few years of life, that Latinx people (usually called Mexicans or Hispanics) were not entitled to our lifestyles. They were servants and farmworkers and, as far as I understood then, they always would be. Things were getting complicated, though, about "the Black race," as I sometimes heard it called.

My world expanded from the kindergarten view, as childhood worlds do (and adult worlds can, if we are lucky). I was stunned the first time I went to work with my father. I was a second-grader then, and he was a professor at an urban community college. I couldn't believe how many people of color were on the campus. It seemed impossible that so many adults wearing big Afros and bright clothes would just come up and speak to my father and he'd respond. And Latinx students too— some dressed in smart assimilation-wear that would please my mother, some wearing heavy eyeliner and styles of which she would not approve. The professors I saw were white—or at least they appeared that way. I didn't yet know that my father's whiteness was, in part, something he constructed to allow him access to this very profession.

It would take me many years to learn why his family, in Texas, was so enamored of me being a "California girl." To them, I possessed a kind of race-class difference that was not accessible to them. Whiteness was very important to my father's mother, and it was connected to the chance for class mobility. Even now, it's hard for me to know which stories were true about our racial history. Her mother's name was Saffronia, a name commonly given to Black women with "high yellow" skin. I look white but grew up with people commenting on my father's and my skin as being "olive." I'm certainly not white like my mother, who is of English ancestry. On my father's father's side, my great-aunt was Comanche, but my father never told me that we were too. My father wiped the Texas accent from his voice entirely when he moved to California to attend university and then graduate school. He was handsome and learned fashion and style. He became "exotic." A word I eventually took to mean that we were white enough. Whiteness in the United States is performative, and that first day at the community college I saw how vibrant my culture's performances of race can be.

I was told to stay in my father's office when he had to step away. Or I could go next door to visit his kind female colleague. She had a jar of lemon drops on her desk and offered them to me on my infrequent visits. I remember feeling confused to learn that she was also a professor, not a secretary, as I had originally assumed. She was white, and her office looked just like my father's, but surely she wouldn't also be a professor.

Scripts about gender and race and how people should look and interact were already embedded in my psyche. I recall them and speak and write about them. We don't just throw away one script in favor of new ones. We have to manage all of them. I also have stories about choosing to revise my parents' values. Those revisions are critical for all of us—and I hope to be an active participant, so that I improve my ability to revise throughout my life. It's foolish to decide what's what and then carry on as though it will always be so. For instance, I recall being a young teenager in the car with my mother when she said, "that big Black booger needs to stay over there," regarding a man on a corner as we drove past. She locked her door upon seeing him, and her word choice taught much about how I should perceive his humanity. I had already been questioning her views and language choices, and I committed myself to not being racist by locking the door or clutching at my purse just because a person of color was near. I also remember deciding that I would likely still protect myself in a sexist environment by locking the car door around men of any race. That decision was based on my real experiences of abuse and male entitlement; they were different than my mother's generalized fear of Black men.

Are these memories, in their embarrassing specificity, hard to hear? Of course they are hard to share; they should be. All of these moments are inside of me. Even when I'm not speaking and writing about racism, they are still there, inside of me, messages about entitlement as a white-privileged, well-educated person, who knows how to dress properly, messages about shame for being fat, for being queer, for being female. Sure, I have grown beyond shame, and the stories live inside me nonetheless, as they live inside each person. We must decide what to do with them. We must handle them when they play back unbidden.

Socialization is not as simple as absorbing our parents' views and values, though our early feelings of belonging and comfort, often in family, are powerful. It's not as simple as absorbing what's on television either, though media can offer us representations to contemplate—like *The Jeffersons*. They can expose us to voices we may not otherwise hear. It was *The Phil Donahue Show* on which I first heard actual people of color speak of their own lives—not actors but real people who had experiences related to the topic of the show. Often, those people I remember so well for their infrequent appearances on television were speaking of race or poverty—topics I believed belonged to them somehow. Sometimes the show would be about losing a child to war, or the difficulty of recent high school graduates looking for work, and there would be a person of color on the panel speaking of her or his experiences as well. It was through these "issues talk shows" that I came to see people of color as fully dimensional with human qualities I could recognize in my own community. The same is true now, for young people watching public figures who are transgender openly discussing their lives. People like LaVerne Cox, Chaz Bono, and Caitlyn Jenner attest to the complexities and diversities of a group previously invisible to those who don't experience being transgender in the United States. Their differences and similarities are becoming legible, little by little, to those who choose to pay attention. They don't represent all of the diversity but a lot more than what was available on television even ten years ago.

Because we live segregated lives, it becomes easy to self-define as either privileged or oppressed in a certain way and then to think of those we define otherwise as very different. If one thinks of oppressed people as so very separate; it's hard to imagine participating in their oppression. *Those poor, unfortunate people*, one may think, as I was taught to think about those who seemed clearly wronged by specific incidents of racism. Yet even though "those poor unfortunate people" endured injuries that were connected to broader systems, those systems remained invisible. It became possible to carry the small messages that some people are defective, less than, undeserving, incompetent, and likely to blame for their own misfortune, at the same time that one could say "oh that poor woman" about a specific rape and beating, loss of opportunity, or tragedy.

It might seem amazing that we handle so many competing scripts in our minds every day, except that many people don't actually acknowledge the scripts that upset them and thereby do not take the time to disrupt their socialization consciously. Many people perform the scripts they were given along with another script that simply says, "I'm different than those who are 'like me.' I'm a good person." I carry a veritable quilt of scripts, in my head at any given moment. So do others who have both endured oppression and accepted that they also hold oppressive views toward others. This quilt is the result of many hours of fine stitching, using a magnifying glass. Still, I find holes in my quilt of competing stories that surprise me and prompt me to get out the magnifying glass again and again. To me, this is what it means to be a responsible adult—to find ways that I participate in oppressive systems, despite my better intentions. I look for the places where I have leverage to change the culture for the better.

A white woman in her fifties contacted me recently to ask for my help in "growing beyond" her familial understanding of race. She felt frightened to say it and said it plainly nonetheless: "I'm a racist." Many in her family are racists. Some belong to white supremacy organizations. She has tried to be "color-blind" because she no longer holds those belief systems, yet she feels those values welling up in her at different times. She doesn't know who to talk to about this—so she wrote to me, as white women often do. We had some conversations about how her racism reveals itself, how she colludes with racist systems, and how she might notice her own thinking, words, and behaviors and choose again. Of course, I suggested that color-blindness was not a worthy aim and offered resources written by Black Americans as well. I have hope for her ability to learn, discern, and add to those stories and experiences she carries. In a country intricately patterned with racism, sexism, homophobia, et cetera, we can't extract those experiences and values from our own lives, but we can add to them and strengthen our resolve to create culture based on other views. We can come into close proximity with as many diverse stories as possible. We can consume a variety of media. We can seek out integrated housing and schooling. We can point out aspects of our national history that have been hidden, such as how redlining and predatory lending practices—bank and government policies—have curtailed the accumulation of wealth for people of color. We can wonder aloud and discuss how that happened and how it coincided with other policy changes that may have seemed unrelated at the time. If we don't discuss recent history, policy choices, the entry points for change remain hidden. Much as the Black Lives Matter protests against police violence of 2020 have forever changed the ways in which we are capable of discussing public safety, policing, and community needs for safety, we can discuss every topic that has been infused with race in America. That is to say, we can discuss what everyday life looks like in the United States. from a variety of perspectives because we don't all live by the same rules and under the same expectations.

Though I work with these issues, sometimes I can't figure out how to do what's right or what feels natural. Do I talk about a thing or not talk about it, offer condolences or take responsibility, show emotion or hide it because it's not my place to take up more space? I don't always know what to do because the ways we have done things up until this very moment, as a culture, offer no map. I have sometimes offended people in my fumbling.

It makes sense that people of color are sometimes fatigued by white fumbling and outraged by the persistence of racism. People need space for outrage and time for rest regarding topics and interactions that can kill through a thousand small cuts. It makes sense that fat people don't want to explain again why the norm of "diet talk" in public places is absolutely gross and can make one want to stay home. It makes sense that transgender people feel hostile when they must constantly correct the pronouns used to describe them. No one wants the job of constant caretaker. Yet progress means fumbling. We are called upon—all of us—to find compassion and good humor, even when we've had to do it too often. I see so much unkindness these days—especially on the Internet, where people feel more entitled to berate one another's imperfections. I worry that the urge to vent justified anger is a habit that leads to domination too. It's a habit that fuels anger. It's not just that we should be careful with others because it's the right thing to do. We must be careful with ourselves to avoid becoming that which we claim to deplore.

Not only do I write and speak about these topics publicly, like my father, I am also a college professor. I have often told students that I see myself this way: I am a racist—and I'm also an anti-racism educator. Their mouths gape, as if they can't believe I've said those despicable words: I am a racist. I'm also sexist, I tell them. Then they really pay attention, because I'm a woman. I'm also homophobic, and the list goes on. These are the values the culture has instilled in me, and they are not the sum of my identity. I have become much more than judgment and blind adherence to the systems in which we live. If I'm lucky and diligent, I tell them, I'll spend the rest of my life unlearning what my culture has taught me about human hierarchy. I hope others help me in ways that nurture my inclusion and ability to revise my own life and participate in the positive revision of our collective culture. I hope to help others, even as I remain flawed. Of course I tell my students these things. They need to know they can do it too.

5.

MOTHERS AND MISFIRES

My father died courteously a few years ago. We stayed in touch through the period of his decline. I visited as often as I could, and he seemed grateful for my company. There was never any particular beef between us; he was mostly absent when I was a kid. Lots of dads hung around the periphery of their children's lives in the sixties and seventies. When I told him we should talk about him not living alone any longer, he said he understood. The following day, he told me he was checking into a nursing home to rehabilitate himself. I was baffled but already had plans to see him in a week. We'd work it out then. He waited for me, health declining. We both knew no "rehabilitation" would occur. When he saw me, he smiled, said he loved me, everything was good, and then he died. Before the next morning. Done.

My mother won't be so easy. She's losing her memory. She's spent all of her money. She's in great physical health and just moved into my house last week. She seems to believe that most things are either my fault for nagging her too much or Barack Obama's fault. This is, at least in part, because he's a Black Democrat Muslim. The worst kind of each of those things.

What happens when the mind begins to misfire? And then a relationship begins to misfire? Rewind. What happens when a relationship misfires and then the mind misfires and—Playback. Misfires create misfires create minds. Forward. Where do we go from here?

Grief washes over me like a storm, like an inconvenience, sometimes like a light summer rain. Grief suddenly raises the level of everything that isn't nailed down, and I gasp for air while trying not to get clocked by the armoire floating by. Grief undoes the buttons on my blouse and nurses like a horrible wailing baby-giant, an ogre-mother-child. Where am I? Under the water or above it? Is this a metaphor or genuine peril? Am I leaving the light on for my child or my mother or myself? I'm afraid of the dark. Maybe we all are. I admit it. I am afraid. We could all be electrocuted, the way I worry the light switch in all this wetness and grief.

The other day, having light conversation with my friend and mother, I made a joke about my friend having done something ridiculous. She said to my mother, with clear sarcasm, "Kimberly's mean."

My mother, in seriousness, with a look of painful resignation on her face said, "I know." She does not see all that I did to love and protect her. She only sees what I did to save myself from her never-ending insatiable need.

During my early twenties, I participated weekly in a peer-facilitated support group for women survivors of sexual abuse and assault. Most of us had survived incest in addition to whatever else. And, sure, we sometimes spoke about our fathers and stepfathers and our mother's boyfriends, uncles or grandfathers. These were the vast majority of abusers. Sometimes we spoke about them. But mostly we talked about our mothers.

Father is a puzzle, no doubt. A puzzle that's sometimes simple, sometimes complex, but all of the pieces are in the box. There's no nefarious rigging of the game. And if you lose a piece, you can just look for it. Father is everywhere and everything. Patriarchy has made father visible. Try to get a job, use language, have sex, open a pickle jar. There's a piece of the puzzle everywhere you look. The puzzle can be solved. Mother is like trying to sculpt fog into usable tools. Even when everything looks right, it doesn't quite work. Everything can dissipate, disappear, or rearrange, leaving you wondering if anything was ever real. I mean, have you lost your mind? Created imaginings? That's how mother is. At least for me.

And what happens when I can't see her anymore? People get old and die. One day turns to the next. The younger are likely to outlive the older. I'm grateful that I know when to cry and just wait for the next good thing to come, even when it's not clear that something good is coming. Something good is always coming.

The best feeling I ever had was right after I gave birth. Relief of pain is a phenomenal high. I didn't understand that something could hurt so badly. I just didn't understand it. I thought childbirth was natural and, because everyone's mother did it, it couldn't be that big a deal. Then I realized that those Lamaze classes were just keeping me distracted and cheerful about the pending disaster, about the earthquake that would rip through my body, turning my bones into tectonic plates that would lurch apart, crash together, tear the soil of me and cause the insides to erupt out. I didn't know how profoundly the body could take over. I've always been a life-of-the-mind kind of gal. I've always relied on the body for pleasure. Okay, I've known pain, and disappointment in the body, but, wow, pleasure. Always and soon, pleasure.

With the birth too, pleasure came when the pain ended. There was so much pain in the core of my body that someone could've walked in and ripped off my arm and I wouldn't have noticed. I kicked a nurse who tried to examine me. And no one would ever peg me for a nurse-kicker. The earth of my body was rending, and she was simply in the way. Trying to put her hand in my vagina to feel the baby's head was profoundly not the right thing for that nurse to do. Pop. Right off the end of the bed she went.

I cried and wailed and felt sure I couldn't push the baby out. But I wasn't the one doing the birthing. My body was becoming an exit wound. When my son arrived, and the doctor lifted the tight little quaking body, the first thing we saw was a stream of urine fountaining from his baby penis. His father, standing by for the magical moment, wept and said, "Aw, he's peeing on you!" I held him briefly, and his father held him briefly. That's when the rush came. A sense of relief from the pain that made me feel all-powerful. A sense of relief from the pain that made me feel like my body was indeed a planet, capable of opening and emitting life and hurtling through space with whole moons in its orbit.

Of course, that feeling was fleeting. I soon slept mightily, no one able to wake me for quite a time after what had been a two and a half day labor. Sleep was too good. Something good is always coming. And then again, something worse.

We spoke of our mothers, mostly. What could be said about the men who sexually abused us as children? We asked each other questions our mothers could not answer. Why did she need him so much? Why did she turn away and tell herself she didn't know? Why did she send him in? Why did she expect me to fix everything, solve everything? Why did she seem so fragile? How could she look at me with such disgust? How could she see me as such a failure? We talked about our mothers.

I didn't let myself know at first that something in my mother's mind was misfiring. My mother had always been cryptic to me, difficult to grasp, harder to hold. After she spent three days visiting my son's small apartment, seeing the sights in his university town—he called to ask me. "Mom, what're you going to do about Grandma?"

"What do you mean 'do about her?'" I said, incredulous.

"She's losing her mind!" he shouted through the phone. And then he recounted her various mental misfires. Not remembering what she ordered in the restaurant, not knowing where she put things in her suitcase, constantly looking for what she'd just set down. And the most disturbing, he said, "Sometimes it seems like she doesn't know who you are."

I am her only child. And she doesn't know who I am.

Sometimes, he said, she seemed to think he was her son and that I was … no one. Yes, I confirmed to him, I had noticed this behavior. Some part of me must've thought it was endemic to our relationship. In the fog of her waking dream, I sometimes recede, inexplicably. I am not visible, not part of the story, not evident in the landscape. Then I return again, as irritating, startling, and as improbable as Barack Obama in the White House. She says she wouldn't be "losing it" if everything weren't so difficult.

What am I going to do about her?

I don't know the answer to that question. I don't know how this story ends. So I'll just make it up.

I'll tell you a mythology that implicates you as well because, whoa, we are all born of imperfect mothers. And enough of them have given good fearlessly that healing the lovelessness of my particular mother, or yours, or me, or our children—this should be easy. We will reach back through time and through our mothers' sadnesses and traumas and broken skin and missed expectations. We will help each angry girl-woman grow up into a whole woman who does her best. We will say: let your insatiability rest. Be whole and full and comfortable. We will do this; and in reaching back, we will feel them reaching forward through us, as they always have been, waiting for a hand to grasp. We will give them our hands and build a monument together from all the good deeds of mothers through time. We will tell them we're sorry for what happened to them as children, as women. We will absolve them of all wrong-doing and tell them they are loved.

That's my story of how this ends. I will care for my mother's body as long as she's in it. Perhaps not as she would most want me to, but I will do it just the same. I will feel both loss and relief when she leaves that body. There have been so many misfires, and now? What could that possibly mean to me now? For her sake and mine, I will care for myself and my body by doing my best. Reaching back through time and death, I will pull us forward, light all of the circuits at once so that the thing I bury, eventually, will be our shame.

6.

TWO A.M.

In my dream last night, I was raising a child in some kind of low-class addict's crash pad. She was a toddler. After I woke up on a mattress on the floor to the sound of some guys setting up a keg on the front lawn, I found her in the bathroom. She'd crawled up onto the sink for a little bath and had her clothes ready to put on. She couldn't have been more than three. She was doing a good job looking after herself.

I realized I didn't know what had happened or whether I'd tended to her at all the day before. She was happy to see me, and my misery was deep. You should've seen the carpet in that place.

• • •

Look, I didn't fuck it up. Not in real life. It was just a dream.

That parenting gig, I didn't fuck it up even remotely. My son didn't spend a minute in a place like that. Not a minute. I wasn't high when I was pregnant, nor when I was raising him. His dad was getting high a lot when I met him, but, by god, he picked right up. He was already picking himself up by the time I got pregnant—okay, we didn't plan that part—but there was no way we were going to mess up something so obviously meant to make us better people. There was just no way. We loved that kid fierce-like from moment one. Then we sent him to college. Follow-through like a medal of honor. I was always grateful to my son's father for seeing things like I did when it came to loving our kid.

Recently, my son told me that his father and I consulted him more often on family decisions than he and his partner ever consult their son. They just tell him what's what. We treated him like he was the prince of the place. We gave him choices, asked for opinions, provided opportunities as fast as most people change the TV channels. We weren't perfect, but we gave the task our attention, our care, that's for sure.

My grandson has opportunities too, but it's different. They decide a thing and lay it down. He goes along. That kid's happy. My son was happy. Sure, he had troubles; it's life. And now he's exhausted; they're parents. They seem like good parents, but they're not precious about it like his father and me. They were both raised in households where nobody was drunk or hitting them or trying to have sex with them when they were kids. Okay, I yelled more than I wish I had, but I didn't belittle him. I apologized. I provided. Lots of things, including lasting love. Maybe that made some difference.

• • •

Before I had the dream, I had been awake and reviewing conversations in my mind with colleagues, with ex-lovers, reviewing things I wish I could say now. Mostly those "can't we just take a look at ourselves?" kind of things that help people have a laugh, reconnect in a loving way, and get on with feeling fine. Damn it, I can't stand not being able to just get on with it. I forgive everything. I mean, I do. I may not trust a person again in the same way after things get shitty. Or I may even decide to trust again. People aren't all one way or another. People have to do what they have to do, be who they are, work out their own stuff. That includes me. I definitely want someone to cut me some slack, keep loving me even if I fuck things up. Mostly, I get back what I give in that regard. Mostly I'm still loved. Mostly.

So, I was up thinking through past conversations, as I do at two a.m. Sometimes I'm reviewing how I'd like to give someone a piece of my mind, but usually it's not an in-your-face kind of piece of my mind. It's more like, Why can't I get you to understand me? Jesus, will you just listen? It's like that. I hate being misunderstood worse than most things, and somehow as soon as people are attracted to each other in some kind of big way, the possibility for misunderstanding skyrockets.

But even when I'm trying to get someone to understand me, it's usually so we can just have a little look at ourselves, have a little laugh and get on with it. I value ease. I value intimacy.

Here's what I don't do at two a.m. nearly as often as I used to: pick up the damn phone and call the person. Send an email. Text or message them looking for a response.

So, at two a.m., I was thinking through what I would say to whom, if only there was someone listening. But even though my mind gets going enough that I can't sleep, something's still all right in there. My mind's not just an evil-carnival-at-midnight, and goodness knows it can be. I've gotten into deep shit in my own head after dark. But not so often anymore. My mind can get going, and still there's that witness part of me that stands off to the side of those head-conversations and offers gentle observations and commentary. She never used to show up at two a.m. I used to have to go find her during meditation or on a long walk or in the calm after a good workout. This feels like progress that she's with me almost all the time now. Not always, but, hey, she even shows up at two a.m. on occasion, and she was with me last night.

She was saying, Wow, look how much you still want to be loved. Look how much you are still playing out the programming of your childhood, in which you longed to be valued and understood, no matter what you looked like. You felt so different, and you just wanted to be known by a few people who got you. You didn't want to feel used for someone else's pleasure or pride or to soothe another's misery. It all makes sense. Look at you now, trying to get the love you want. Good for you, not trying to use others to soothe your misery. Good for you. Good you. Good.

See how that works? The mind that wants to explain something to others and make me seem lovable again? It may still do that, and now it explains that stuff to me too.

Look, it's been decades since I've spent time in those misery hovels where people are broke and getting high and neglecting their kids and eating Taco Bell for dinner again. *Holy shit*, I recall thinking once. *That guy's eaten nothing but Taco Bell for, like, thirty years. How is he still alive?* I mean, that was never, even remotely going to be my life. The witness in me knew it wasn't going to happen, yet I stood on that carpet enough times. Carpet that's been puked on and dried up and scrubbed every few years by somebody's new girlfriend, and worn through and plywood's showing underneath and who could give one shit because the landlord never—I mean never—comes to even have a quick look. In my dream, I looked down at my feet on that carpet, and the scent of piss came back like it was yesterday. I still look down at my feet on that carpet, and it feels like something I deserve. Sometimes I feel a rage when that happens. Sometimes I just feel small.

My god, when I saw her giving herself a bath in the sink and realized that I had fucked up, the pain was almost unbearable.

In the waking hours, the real time, the day-living in which all of the actual things happen, I don't fuck things up. I don't let people down. I've done things lovers didn't like; I've left. But I've never lied about fucking around or disappeared or stolen from someone I loved or made the slightest vindictive move toward anyone when I've felt wronged. I've felt wronged, and I've yelled about it. I can ride a sarcastic tone off into the sunset, but yippee-i-ay, I always hope someone comes looking for me there, sitting by my campfire sobbing, sarcasm sleeping in the sagebrush.

Sure, there may have been times when I could've done more to keep a friend from going off with that guy who raped her or to talk someone out of an abusive relationship, but that's hindsight stuff. That's in the probably-wouldn't-have-worked-anyway category of things that might've been. I always did my best. I always pulled up out of my own pain on behalf of others.

Sometimes I didn't even take the drugs so I could look after the wasters in my company. Like that time I pocketed a hit of acid at the last minute when everyone else dosed because, wow, traffic. It's like we were dropping acid in the middle of a racetrack. I was stoned, but then that wore off, and I acted as babysitter for the next eight hours, and no one walked into the headlights on my watch. That's just how I was. How I am. Always thinking it through.

Even still sometimes, I'm afraid. I'm afraid I could still be to blame for something. Two a.m. me is particularly suspicious. Maybe I think I have it together, but I really don't. I want to be better than everyone else. (Because, let's face it, how easy will *that* be?) I also want to learn to let it rest. It's tiring. I do okay. And it's tiring.

At two a.m., the witness asked me, Will you always be trying to prove you're worthy of love? Or can you just accept love?

And I paused, in whatever review-of-the-pain I was conducting and said, Shit man, I don't know.

That witness, she's kind. She's patient. No matter what.

Then there was enough spaciousness in my head to allow sleep. But that dream came. And when I woke, I shed a few tears, shook my head, and thought, *wow.* The fear of forgetting, the fear of fucking up, is long and wide and deep and maybe sometimes useful. It's like a wound that doesn't close. A long, beautiful blood-lake you could sail under the light of a full moon. Like a tear in the earth after a volcano erupts, making new land.

7.

TRIGGER WARNINGS AND THE MYTH OF OVERSENSITIVE STUDENTS

My mother has always had a big dog as her companion. Purebred, large, and obedient. Currently, it's a standard poodle, before that a Bouvier and a German Shepherd. When I was growing up, there was a Norwegian Elkhound, a Samoyed, and an Old English Sheepdog.

One might say she loves dogs. I think she'd say so too. It may be more accurate to say she loves *having* a dog—and I'm not sure the two are the same thing.

When I was about twelve, a Doberman darted out in front of the car when my mother was driving. We weren't far from our home and moving slowly, single-file in traffic. We both shrieked when the car struck the dog, and I carry a visceral memory of the back wheels lifting, bones cracking as we drove over the dog's ribcage. My mother began sobbing and repeating a shrill "My god. My god. My god."

The dog must've just come off the leash or out of a yard because the owner was there in an instant, at the back window of our car, looking to care for the dying dog. I don't know if he blamed her or not. When I started to roll down the window, my mother screamed for me to leave it up. I was stunned that her horror about the dog turned so quickly to anger at me.

See, I thought we were going to stop the car and attend to what had happened. We didn't. She drove on, muttering, "I can't. I can't. I can't. I can't." And then the rest of the day, I heard her tell the story of the horrible thing that happened to *her* that morning, in running over the dog.

Schooled as I was in hysterical outbursts, my initial response was to twist my body around to look at the people hovering over the dying dog. I shrieked, "You have to stop! It's not right! We have to go back! We have to." But as usual, her denial won the day, and she was the one driving. I soon fell silent as she sobbed, "I can't. I just can't." I understand that we also experienced a significant event, but I felt more damaged by her early departure, her inability to see a tragedy through to grief and sadness, rather than cutting it short with denial.

Not quite fifteen years later, when her German Shepard was ill, she handed the leash off to my husband to handle her dog being euthanized, again muttering, "I can't. I just can't." I can think of other, minor incidents of passing off tasks that simply didn't seem ladylike to accomplish. That's what I thought at the time. There were things that, with a man around, she simply shouldn't have to do.

She may enjoy *having* a dog, but there's a peculiar lack of evidence that she feels something as deep, complex, and abiding as love.

I had already given thought to "trigger warnings" when the University of Chicago passed a ruling in August 2016 declaring that professors should no longer use them on campus. I've never used this term in my syllabi and don't when I teach. And yet, for many of us explicitly feminist educators, social scientists, and humanities professors who handle the stuff of everyday life, namely the contours of privilege and oppression, we are aware that people have been hurt. They will be triggered by our themes of study.

Students deserve our respect and gentleness. I tell them specifically that we will be discussing difficult themes when I teach courses such as Body and Identity or Race and Inequality or Marriage and the Family. I tell them that they should look after themselves and offer some suggestions on how to do that, though certainly non-prescriptively.

Most importantly, I tell them that I'll do my level best to create an environment that allows for respectful disagreement, exploration of difficult topics, and, still, I won't allow any groups or individuals to be belittled—even those who we think are not in the room with us. I also tell them that I can make mistakes too and need to be questioned on occasion.

I revisit these messages as often as needed as we navigate material that is at turns difficult, enlightening, entertaining, fascinating, and challenging. I do it in order to keep people in the conversation, not to give them an easy escape route.

Let's be careful with language. I want everyone to know where the escape route is on a topic they simply can't handle any more on a certain day or in a certain way. Sometimes, when images are involved in our study of violence, for instance, I give alternate assignments. I want to build an environment that makes it easier to stay in the room when things are difficult. That's the part over which I have some control: the culture and environment of learning.

My explicit aim is to enact a pedagogy of love in which transformation is always an option—for the students, for me, and, if we continue our studies and active creation of culture, for the society itself. Love requires presence. It's deep and complex and not always capable. When I have a student who wants to opt out of discussing a certain topic, or is simply checked out, not paying attention, and I can't tell why, that student retains my respect. I also want to know—especially if a student is concerned about grades—how they have engaged with our themes of study. Needing to turn away from a topic of study in a particular moment does not mean failing to consider it deeply at some point.

Much as my mother turned to me with anger when I challenged her decision not to attend to what she'd done by running over the dog, it's easy for professors to turn quickly to students as the source of irritation when we are questioned. It's easy because, often, they are the ones revealing a problem, suggesting that something in our approach be slowed or diverted. Professors, due to institutional and personal constraints, often feel seriously challenged when asked to slow down or reroute.

Sometimes, I find student desire to opt out problematic. I have had students claim they shouldn't have to read a book that contains "so much" profanity, for instance. I've had students claim they shouldn't have to discuss queer families because it's wrong and goes against their religion. Students. Plural. On both of these topics, female students have claimed that these kinds of assignments should be optional. I've also had male students simply check out of discussions and assignments dealing with pornography and rape. I've had white students check out in discussions dealing with racism. In these latter cases, the disconnect happens without verbal pre-planning, but if I inquire about the check out I hear that those topics are just "too much." I see heads shaking and—do I imagine it? Eye rolling.

In considering who is damaged enough by a topic not to want to discuss it, often it's those who don't want to examine their own positions of power or privilege, who feel they "shouldn't have to" engage. This is very different from feeling triggered by past trauma.

See, it's possible to want very much to be in school and yet not to have a love of learning. As with my mother's relationship with dogs, it's possible that "I can't" can really mean "I shouldn't have to."

For some students, the trigger warning is a way to stay in the discussion, to know what's coming, to look after oneself. For others, it means, "Whew, I don't have to talk about this, because it's uncomfortable."

Why do professors and policies like the one at University of Chicago seem to focus more on this latter interpretation? In my experience, it is the more rare. Literally every student who stays *in* the conversation benefits from a classroom environment that honors their discomfort and helps them plan ahead.

In her article, "Against Students" Sara Ahmed cautions us to pay attention to the broad sweeping statements made against students who seem "over-sensitive." I agree wholeheartedly with her that "over-sensitive can be translated as: Sensitive to that which is not over." She says, "The idea that students have become a problem because they are too sensitive relates to a wider public discourse that describes *offend-ability* as a form of moral weakness and as a restriction on "our" freedom of speech. Much contemporary racism works by positioning the others as too easily offendable, which is how some come to assert their right to occupy space *by being offensive*."

The difficult truth is that not all professors are setting up a culture of respect and environments of study that are conducive to deep and respectful learning. Neither do the systems within universities support those kind of classrooms, and the institutions themselves often seem more interested in profit and prestige than anything else.

Do some get it right? Absolutely, right down to the administration that supports learning. (Note, I didn't say "up.")

There are instructive (and often predictable) patterns in who feels they shouldn't have to discuss certain topics, just as there are patterns in the types of folks who hold systems accountable to respectful practices. We have to make time and sometimes challenge ourselves to attend to those patterns.

We also have to navigate a good amount of ambiguity as both creators and responders in learning environments. Sometimes when systems are damaged—when professor pay is inadequate, when sexual harassment is the protected standard, as two examples—it can feel like we're repairing the ship as we steer through a storm. Guiding people's learning about difficult topics is a challenging job under great circumstances. There are no simple fixes here. We need presence, accountability, and respect. Sometimes we need patience, sometimes urgency.

To add complexity, it's definitely possible for professors to be committed to feminist education or anti-racism education and still not have all of the tools and relationships sorted out well enough to prevent seeing "overly sensitive" students as a problem. We should always see it as an instructive thing—as events worthy of contemplation and action. Similarly, the responses we receive from students regarding "trigger warnings" can teach us something.

There are also patterns in faculty responses to student requests for sensitivity. These responses require a more immediate intervention. Under no circumstances should accusations of sexual harassment or racism be re-coded as student sensitivity. When we see that and tolerate it—and even when we hear students comment on it, or read in social scientific studies that it is likely occurring even when we don't see it—then we are letting down our responsibility as educators.

Sensitivity is good. Even if we don't know what to say or do immediately, it's wise to continue pondering situations that don't "feel" right without labeling them too quickly. We can find trusted colleagues (preferably across institutions) with whom to discuss situations for perspective. We can reject any interpretation that seems to valorize how things were done in a previous time period without being clear about who benefited from those circumstances.

Dear student, how will you attend to what needs attending to in the subject matter, even if you can't attend class on a certain day, or you can't do a certain assignment? This is my question. I ask the same of myself, my colleagues regarding our responsibility to engage liberatory pedagogy and attend to student concerns. I question the support of the institutions in which I am implicated, whose work I perpetuate. I remind myself that I am capable of applying what I've learned and that I am not beholden to institutions; we are co-creating our relationship. I'm not a traumatized child screaming in the car about injustice and the failure of love. I understand something about power imbalances and accountability. And I'm capable of learning more. Scholars like Ahmed help me, and hopefully we both help others.

I've witnessed and sometimes suffered from my mother's failings. I've also experienced love and nurturing from her. The systems in which we work, as teachers, can both nurture and abuse us as well. It's a complex relationship. Of course, we do well to remember that we are not children at the whim of adults whom we must please or risk destruction. It's not enough to shut the office door and look after ourselves when things get too hard. That's just surviving. And although we "shouldn't have to" engage deeply with the flaws of our institutions, it is part of the work we've taken on to do.

8.

UNLOVABLE

If you've ever felt certain you're not lovable, come on over. Sit by me.

I was walking up the steps toward the bank. The sun was hitting the glass door so that I couldn't see inside. I guess the woman coming out didn't see me either, and—bam—the big glass-and-wood door clocked me in the face. I stumbled back a bit, head throbbing. We both said *oh shit*, she apologized, and I shook it off, got on with the day. My nose wasn't broken, but I had a black eye for a week.

When I saw my sweetie the following day, she assessed the damage gently in public, and then later in bed she cozied up next to me. "Goddamn, you're even hotter when you've been roughed up a bit." She kissed me and pushed her head against mine, making me wince in pain. "Mmm," she grunted.

"You're one sick fucker." We both laughed.

"Yeah, at least I'm not the one who hit you. Count your blessings I'm mostly over that shit." We shook our heads and laughed again.

Look, no part of me wants pain. I understand how pain can be cathartic, and it's not my thing. I always talked myself out of a beating, smelled the metal of my own blood through the skin before it broke, and got myself out of there. I don't attract the ones who hit, but I sure attract the ones who could. And I learn how not to push. Being careful not to get hit, apparently that's my gig. And I'm good at it.

In my youth, I had a flair for the flamboyant outburst. I mean, I was never one of those jealous glass throwers; I never upset a table in a restaurant. I'm not violent at all, just a little loud. Even still today,

I'll yell and put on the Medusa face, but I do it in the privacy of my home.

This was my last big scene and how it finally clicked that I was done with that nonsense.

We'd been upstairs at my place, having sex and then arguing about some damn thing. I couldn't begin to say what. She was visiting for the weekend and decided, no, fuck it, she was leaving. I was wearing a pale green and cream lace silky negligee with a little pearly business along the bodice. That I remember clearly. She threw all of her stuff in the duffle bag and heaved it onto her shoulder and went down the stairs. I followed, giving her a piece of my mind every step of the way. Fire was shooting from my eyeballs as I watched her step off the porch and head down my steep front yard into the dark night. I shouted one last thing, loud enough for her to hear as she got into her truck: "YOU ARE ONE FUCKED-UP INDIVIDUAL!"

And suddenly that thing happened. A zoom out. An awareness. Suddenly a small, but terribly clear voice inside my head said, "Actually, you are standing on *your* front porch at two a.m., yelling for *your* neighbors to hear, wearing nothing but a skimpy negligee. You have just become the dictionary illustration for 'one fucked up individual.' Why don't you close your mouth and go in the house?"

And I went in the house.

She sat in the car for ten minutes, and then I heard her mumbling angrily, hauling her bag up the stairs, bump by bump, then telling me, as she took off her clothes and got in bed, "Goddammit, if I leave now, I can't fuck you again in the morning."

At which I rose up briefly like a cobra to say, "Oh, so you think we're having sex in the morning?"

And she said, "Shut up. Just shut up. Go to sleep." There wasn't much fight left in me, so I did.

Yeah, we had sex in the morning.

She never hit me, but after a few disturbing episodes of almost, she went back to anger management classes and I joined a domestic violence abuse survivors' support group. Things weren't always good between us, but that relationship lasted a decade because we both had fix-it tenacity. We tried to better ourselves this way and that. And now, years later, as friends, we love each other still.

Maybe that's all I will ever have in the relationship department. Love.

Not comfort. But love. What a strange consolation prize.

I sure know how to pick 'em. And they pick me just as surely. Okay, sometimes different people try to pick me, but I just don't get the hots for too many people, and I send them straight to the friend zone. With some, there's a fast hard click, like a metal lock. That kind of connection rarely slips out of place until we've moved through some serious business together. How do we know even before we know? Is it scent or aura or the hand of God that shoves us together on the sofa?

I was talking to a recent unsuitable suitor on the front porch. We were drinking wine and smoking cigars, and I said, "Hey, look, don't you even get it going for me! I mean, you don't want the likes of me. I am damaged and downright difficult. I mean, fuck sake, you were raised by nice people in middle-class suburbia, and you've worked at the same job for thirty years. What the fuck? Stay away from me."

I say no more often than I say yes. The body has to choose; my head can't be in charge. It's a little fucked up in there where mating's involved. The circuits didn't get laid quite right in the beginning, maybe. Though I give advice to others like a champ, keep my head cool in most situations, I rarely know what to tell myself. It's not like I'm pre-interviewing lovers—the fact is, I rarely get a lady-boner for people who haven't had the crap beat out of them a few times when they were kids. It was probably someone who loved them doing the beating.

One could say, well, that's just common. And it'd be true. But there are similarities among most of my lovers that are downright eerie. Probably it's comfortable for me. Probably it's familiar to me. Probably it fits somehow with something I learned when I was a kid. Isn't what the therapists would say?

I pick people who are too damaged to trust anyone fully by the time they get to me. Maybe the part of me that thinks I'm not lovable says that seems right. I don't deserve trust and comfort. But it makes me mad. And they're so certain they can't be loved that my anger seems deserved. But it also justifies the lack of trust.

That's it. Those are the ones I'm hot for.

Or maybe it looks like this: I'm so calm and accepting, I seem like a miracle at first. Truly, I am calm and accepting and a motherfucking miracle as well, but you've got to know that some anxious lovelessness caused me to pursue all that calm, and as soon as you upturn the table, you're gonna see how it was made. I can't get to the sex without showing someone how I'm made. Well, I can't get to it more than once or twice, and I'm a more than once or twice kind of gal.

My lovers usually can't let down their guard. They can't be honest with themselves about how they keep creating their own misery despite trying really hard to get clear, meditate, breathe, get back to nature, journal, join a tantra group, talk to a shrink, and get freaky, at least for a while, with me. I have some kind of mojo going on that keeps them wanting the sex, that's for sure.

It's a shame one can't put a nozzle on one's own mojo, point it in the right direction, build it up, and let it fight the fire of a painful past. My lovers are fighters with mojo to spare, but it's not clear whether we're ever fighting in the right direction. I like 'em either super-scrappy or super-smart; both is best. What if we could point ourselves toward those painful pasts together, rather than looking right at each other when we're mad?

After years of on again and off again, my lover with the anger issues and I went to couples counseling. After some time talking about our problems with sex—that is, talking about how she loves fucking me but doesn't totally let me do her, she said this to the therapist: "I just know that if I really soften up with her, it'll be the best thing ever. Then I'll need it. Then she can hurt me."

I wept quietly because, yeah, I knew that. She didn't want me to have the power to withdraw my love or leave her. They're not always the same thing. I also knew she was already in pain without me doing the hurting. A pain I couldn't touch because it had installed such anger inside of her, I couldn't get close. I guess she figured it was easier not to heal, to keep the low-grade fever of anger and hunger. Better to blame me for not trying hard enough.

Pain is easier to carry than fear. Both will shorten your life. Whatever. We're resilient as fuck, my lovers and I. That much is clear.

I have to hope for something better. It could be worse, and it's not. I pick someone with a few skills. I don't pick the ones who are strung out on drugs. I don't pick the ones who hit. I just pick the ones who need love and won't accept it from me. Maybe a little they do. Small morsels. But I don't do a good job pretending it's enough. There's a lot of fighting to be loved here on my side of the table. A lot of trying and failing. A lot of tear-it-down-and-try-again hope. A lot of joy despite the pain. Real eye-of-the-storm peace. A lot of tenacity and tenderness because there doesn't seem to be another way. I have known lasting love, but sometimes the romantic relationship has to end to get there.

If you've ever felt certain you're not lovable, come on over. Sit by me.

There are a lot of you out there. Just like how I learned to stop making a screaming scene on my own front porch, maybe I can learn to draw someone with a softer jaw, an unclenched fist. That's possible. And here's what's likely: No matter who sits by me, I'll keep pouring up love by the cupful. Sweet love. No matter what else happens, that's not nothing. Love is never going to be nothing.

9.

THE BODY POLITIC

"For myself, 'survivor' contains its other meaning: one who must bear witness for those who foundered; try to tell how and why it was that they, also worthy of life, did not survive. And pass on ways of survival; and tell our chancy luck, our special circumstances."

—Tillie Olsen, *Silences*

December 2017

Just. Can't. Do it.

Like a cat going into a bath twists this way and that. You want to push this? Someone gets hurt. Better I pull off the freeway and not push it. I can't make my foot go down onto the gas pedal.

Ohio in October was the beginning of the end. A bridge popped up out of nowhere. I was already having trouble staying above fifty miles per hour on the freeway, and there it was. Everyone was going at least sixty-five and I slowed to about twenty in heavy traffic, flicked on the hazards. I actually thought it'd be easier to drive over the edge of the bridge than to stay with the feeling of terror. I couldn't keep up. "No," I said to myself aloud. "No, you are going to get to this university and do the event. You are going to have dinner with students and make it to the Cleveland airport tomorrow. You are going to see your son in Chicago. That's all you have to do. Go see your son and your grandson." My own voice talking in the car, convincingly, got me across.

From that point on, I didn't attempt it anymore. No more driving on freeways. What had been difficult for more than a year became impossible.

That night, near midnight, I let the GPS guide me through every small road in Ohio from Oxford to Cleveland. Across a small, lower bridge, I drove alone. After that, no more bridges either. And anything where I could see an embankment to the right, I couldn't do it. Or really any long left-curving road. Not that either. I thought the therapy in spring had been helping, but it wasn't helping enough. I thought maybe the *ho'oponopono* would have an ancillary effect.

September 2017

Mostly, he laughs and listens and stops me when I say something useful. "Hey, wait a minute!" he yells, bright eyed. "Take a deep breath; say that part again." After I do, he says excitedly, as though listening to a good story, "Okay, what else?"

I have come for a ho'oponopono session because the worry I have for my son and my mother is preventing me from sleeping. Ho'opono-pono is the process of making things right. You don't need someone's permission or even participation to make things right. The people with whom you want to make things right don't even need to be alive. You can do it all by yourself. Say this:

I'm sorry.

Please forgive me.

Thank you.

I love you.

You can do ho'oponopono with the help of a kahuna, a guide. I am crying all the time, and I can't sleep, and driving with others on the road has become so hard. I live in Hawaii, where ho'oponopono is the indigenous way of helping. I work often in North America where freeways abound. I know I need help.

My mother is losing her memory and may not have enough money to make it through the rest of her days. She is incorrigible and won't accept any help from me that would make any kind of sense. She won't move into the downstairs apartment at my house. She won't give up her Lexus and her giant poodle's visits to the fancy groomer twice a month. She voted for Trump and thinks everything should be okay now that he won. She's losing her memory and knows that something is wrong. She can't afford her mortgage and needs to move out of her house. I don't even know her full financial situation. I can't help her because she won't allow it.

My son has a good job, better than most. He has health insurance and a modest pension. He works for a university, but, he reminds me, his adjusted income is less than mine was when I was his age, with less education and a job with less status. He reminds me of this because he thinks I judge him poorly. He is twenty-seven with tremendous debt. His father and I paid for his bachelor's degree, but he took out loans for the master's degree. He hears judgment in everything I say, and he is constantly anxious about providing for his family. His partner looked for work for two years. Their son knows a middle-class lifestyle, but what does that even mean anymore? He is taking medication for the anxiety. When they finally split up and he moves into a two-bedroom apartment he can ill-afford, I wonder if he should've gotten a studio. An adult and a child can live in a studio apartment, I reason silently. It's not pleasant, but it's honest. Maybe I am judging his decisions in addition to judging the economic circumstances my nation has created. I cannot help him, and I cannot sleep at night. He takes anxiety medication and rants on the Internet about how cisgender white men have ruined everyone's life. He is a cisgender white man, painfully woke.

"You're gonna light a candle for your mother and one for your son. You're gonna ask God to take care of them because you've done all you can do." I nod, tears streaking my face. Near the end of the session, the kahuna says, "How're you feeling? Anything physical I can help with?" I shrug, but he looks expectantly. "You got a rash?" he finally asks, as though I've forgotten, which I have. The rash seems so minor in comparison to the worry for my son and my mother.

"I do," I say matter of factly. "In my armpit. Since the election."

"Right," he says, as though that was the answer he was looking for. He jumps up and goes to the kitchen, comes back with a mason jar full of bright yellow creamy liquid and a giant avocado. "Take a sip of that," he says. I do and he watches my face. "Is it good?" he says. I nod. "Good!

You take a jar of this, turmeric, sea salt, coconut milk. And you drink it in one day, with a whole avocado. You gonna feel some things move!"

My eyes widen, and he laughs again. "No gotta be weird about it. Just have some avocado on toast in the morning, on a salad at lunch. Pau. You ate a whole avocado. Don't have to sit there with a spoon and eat it all at once!" He laughs uproariously. "You gotta tree with fruit at home?" I nod. "Great!" He exclaims, "you don't need my avocado. That'll take care of the rash but not the president. Need more than avocados for that!" I nod sadly. Somehow, we didn't even talk about the driving.

February 2017

It happened once before. I just couldn't bring myself to accelerate on the freeway. The cars were closing in. My hands went numb and my vision tunneled. What the hell? I used to drive cross-country, sixteen hours a day on the freeway, no problem. Suddenly, I couldn't do freeways and bridges.

That's how the body is: totally in charge. I can forget this fact, act like it isn't true, and sometimes that ruse takes hold for a while. I'd say in my mind, Just accelerate and pass this car. My numb hands and unresponsive pedal-foot would reply, *Bow down before the body, foolish thinker. You may be chatty, but you're not in charge.*

It happened to my father during the few years before his death. He couldn't go on the freeway, even as a passenger. Once a large man, his body had shrunk. His hands and knee joints seemed enormous against his shrinking limbs.

We never spoke of it directly, but I saw his fear. He'd get in the car for me to take him to the doctor, and he'd immediately tell me which route to take. No freeways. I'd just shrug and say sure, but suddenly, when he died, I couldn't drive on the freeway either. I didn't put it together on my own, but my friend remembered his fear and said, "Grief comes out in strange ways." I hadn't thought of it, but somehow that felt right.

Now it's back. I can't stand anyone driving next to me at a speed over thirty miles an hour. After my father died, I struggled with that driving anxiety for about a year and then, poof, it was gone. I felt fine again, like nothing had ever been wrong. Halfway through 2016, when Donald Trump was on every TV monitor in every public place, sounds of his recorded voice in every broadcast, I suddenly couldn't drive in traffic again. My father died more than six years ago, but when the anxiety came back, I knew it wasn't him. It was Donald.

Why do people keep handing him a microphone? Why does the news keep showing up at his events? That's what I kept wondering when I'd see him. When he received the Republican nomination, it still didn't make sense. And then it did. Something I had not taken the time to understand fully enough had blindsided me. And now, I become frightened in a part of me that the chatty mind can't control. The body and the mind are communicating below the radar of my awareness. Who are all those people in those cars? I don't know them. They could do anything at any moment. None of us are safe. Somehow I know, in a non-language way, that the rise of Donald Trump's popularity is driving my inability to drive.

To be clear, I am still driving. I'm not stalled and sweating in the driveway. I have to drive to a university and teach three days a week after all. I have to. An hour each way and no reliable public transportation or carpools to be had. I've searched online, asked friends. So I drive. I'm just slow, unsafe. I need to stay in the far right lane where no one can get on the right side of me. Sometimes I get off the road and breathe, cry, rest. I arrive everywhere in a sheen of perspiration, my chest aching and my body withered with exhaustion. I breathe through it. When I can switch the channel in my mind to thinking "we're all just moving in the same direction together" or even "life is a grand mystery and mostly we're fine." it gets better. Until it gets worse again.

It's not like I didn't understand that racism has always been a profound motivator in politics. Or sexism or homophobia. People become afraid that they aren't getting as much as they deserve. Indeed, they're not getting as much as the culture promises. Then fear drives the ballot. Keep the immigrants away. White men and white families should get theirs first. It's an undercurrent in the body, even when the mind can't quite articulate the pull. As soon as he had the nomination, I felt the possibility of election, and I remained watchful, ever watchful of what was whizzing by on either side of me.

My son was born during the height of the AIDS crisis. Politicians were threatening concentration camps for gay people, and I was afraid my son could be taken from me and his father because of our queerness. A distant fear, but a fear nonetheless. His dad and I, though we were both queer, were married to each other. On paper, we looked like a "normal" family, and that gave me some small comfort. Still, as a writer and human rights activist, it would've been easy enough to target us if it had come to that. Thankfully, it didn't come to that. I don't recall any body-anxiety back then. I don't recall any rash or difficulty sleeping or driving.

Oh yeah, the rash. I've never had skin problems. At first I thought it was a rash, but it was a yeast infection. Cortisol released into the body at high levels when I drive can apparently reduce immune functioning and elevate blood sugar. That often causes candida overgrowth. Yeast infection.

At an academic conference in November, right after the election, a woman spoke on this topic during an ad hoc meeting in which a group of feminist scholars were discussing responses to the election. This woman urged self-care. And when she mentioned candida overgrowth, I wasn't the only one in the room nodding knowingly.

The body remembers and makes associations. Now that I recall, now that my mind recalls, I can tell you I had yeast infections as a young adolescent, right before I broke away from my incest-supporting home.

Notice how I word that? My incest experience was not just about a thing my stepfather did to me in private. I lived in an incest-supporting culture that was organized around my incest-supporting home. The body keeps the score. I left that home in order to make a new life, a countercultural life to supplant the one I had been given. My repertoire for living and learning is large, and, still, the body holds everything in a tight weave. Nothing escapes the understanding of skin and muscle. I am starting to see, by which I mean feel, that there is something wonderful about this cumulative wisdom, even though I can't get to work well-rested these days. Something's happening that feels too familiar. Yet I am not young. I am capable. I am knowledgeable. I don't have clear language for this driving problem yet, but I know the body has taken care of me before.

When I was thirteen, my stepfather would sometimes take me to the country club where he played golf, and the men there seemed to know something about me. At least they thought they did. I didn't look like a child, and a lot can be assumed about someone young who doesn't look like a child. A girl who looks like a woman draws assumptions like flies. The rash, the sleeplessness—that feeling again, like being at the country club with my stepfather and realizing suddenly that everyone's in on the joke about my lack of worth. Blindsided.

Hillary Clinton almost won. Some say she did, because of the popular vote, but that's not how we choose a president. I went online to see what I could find about the electoral college voters, and most were already Trump supporters. There would be no overthrow of the system. The fact of her near win caused some to double down on their sexism, so that it leaked out in public interactions with strangers. Men sneered more often; my friend said a well-dressed man on a city sidewalk looked straight at her as he refused to share the space. He nearly shoved her off the curb and it felt like part of a pattern. This kind of sexism can live in our bodies, not just in our minds and mouths.

It's not that America's sexism is stronger than its racism. It's just harder to see in certain ways. Most people live in two-gender households, work in two-gender jobs. We are constantly in semi-civil contact, rigid rules in place to ensure the functioning of social and familial systems so that the weft and the warp of our national fabric can work together. Whether fashioned of slave cotton or immigrant silk or the hats and ties Trump imports from China, the fabric of oppression won't unravel or tear asunder. Despite what we believe about ourselves as "caring for women" or "not being racist," we are participating in the system as it is, as it has always been.

Most Americans still live in fairly segregated neighborhoods, attend racially segregated schools, so it's easier to create stories about racial others that don't require a lot fancy machinery in the mind to close the weave. This is a problem, to be sure. Our isolation causes stories of the other to go unchallenged by contact. White families don't socialize with Black or Latinx families, so it's harder to see that everyone's kids are "just hanging out" rather than teens of color appearing to be loitering or up to no good when they're in groups. It's harder for those kids to see that just because the white kids are more likely to be in college prep classes, doesn't mean they are any smarter than any group of Black and Latinx students.

Police brutality based on race is easier than that based on gender. If Black and brown bodies always seem to be criminal, their gender is less relevant. Young or old, people of any gender deserve immediate punishment. White men and women are the rightful recipients of police care, even if poverty makes them suspect. In hiring, gender and race function similarly in hierarchy. Race is a problematic construction in the United States, simply a different problem from the one we face with gender.

Regardless of what job she'd have been applying for, Hillary Clinton's qualifications would have been eclipsed by gender. Since she sought a position that only men had ever held in the past, a particular anger was unleashed in our culture. Our sexism is not stronger than our racism, but it's more elaborately hidden, which is saying a lot. As Rebecca Solnit pointed out in her essay "Milestones in Misogyny" (in *Call Them by Their True Names: Crises [and Essays]*) many people seemed infuriated by Clinton's very presence in politics. She discussed how Clinton was accused of not paying enough attention to "the so-called white working class—a term that, given that she wasn't being berated for ignoring women, seemed to be a code word for white men." Allowing any woman to win such an election would've seemed to confirm the domination by women. Sure, people talked about the problem with "intellectuals" and "professionals" trying to overrun "working" people, or "regular" people, in America. Donald Trump has never been a "working" person or in any way "regular," even though he pledged to shake things up. Caring for the poor was always a ruse because the interests of poor women were not part of the equation. The public discourse was always about gender—and specifically women of power and intelligence. Americans don't hate rich men; they succeeded at the game. But intellectuals who have some kind of special knowledge, some kind of inside jokes? Smart women? I'm sure more than a few people got that yeast rash just from watching her on television. Men, of course, but white women too, who couldn't differentiate from the men with whom they build homes and families.

We are not supposed to hear women talk of policies and wars and what they will do with the mantle of power in public. We are not supposed to hear men say the kind of things that Trump was heard on tape saying about grabbing, about entitlement, about women's intimate anatomy. We are in such denial about how it feels to have heard these things, that whichever words felt most threatening went straight to our bodies for deciphering, not to our minds. Sure, we tried to sort out what those words-made-public meant. And then we chose sides. Is it dangerous for people to choose sides as a way to feel safe? Of course it is.

My country has been hostile toward me before—supporting the incest of my family home, threatening to incarcerate me as a disease-carrier and unfit parent. I've often thought about these hostilities as a sociologist, impersonally. Governments and systems are my focus. Suddenly, as people laugh along with Trump's buffoonery and cast their ballots in favor of his "new and different," I can feel how the government is reflected in our bodies, how the fears of our bodies are creating the culture. The culture is us. The people who have imperiled me this time are driving right alongside me on the road. Logically, incest is so much more personal than an election, but no. The animal fear driving the choices of everyone I meet on the street is somehow communicating with the animal fear moistening my own body. It may not be a majority that elected Donald Trump—the groper, the liar, the kind of guy who makes the rape joke with a drink in his hand. Millions voted for him. And I'm as terrified as they are.

November 2016

I fear the highway. Yet I drive. I see the people in their cars, hurtling along on autopilot, thinking about their jobs, their families, singing with the radio. Each of us stewards a vehicle that could cause havoc and death if we made a wrong move and others did not react defensively and immediately. Mobility is freedom. Freeways connect places that would otherwise seem far from each other. My god, I think, as I drive on the freeway, these people could do anything.

Paolo Freire discussed the fear of freedom in people who might otherwise consider themselves awakened. I find myself pondering this possibility in myself: "As Hegel testifies: 'It is solely by risking life that freedom is obtained... the individual who has not staked his or her life may, no doubt, be recognized as a Person; but he or she has not attained the truth of this recognition as an independent self-consciousness.'"

It's easy for me to consider the voting behaviors of those who want to protect their status, their investments, what they believe they've earned. Fearful cowards, I can call them, ignorant of their unearned privileges. As reports emerged, post-election, of more Trump signs on lawns than before the vote, I thought about 'independent self-consciousness." Fear breeds duplicity. The truth is, I know this all too well within my own soft system, my tensing muscles and breathing chest. I am still on the road yet bound by the cloak of the status quo, belted in by the strap of fear. "Fear of freedom, of which its possessor is not necessarily aware, makes him see ghosts."

My father is sitting right beside me, one hand on the car door as if he could steady it. He became so small and frail in his old age. A big man all his life. A big man with big hands and a thick head of hair. He didn't see this small man coming, hair lost, skin like paper, eyes darting with fear and issuing orders about which route to take.

Conclusion

We do not have the power we thought we had. Blindsided. All the credentials or appearances or money or talk of freedom in the world will not bring us safety. How do I become more radical, more clear, more able? The body is preparing me by showing me my fear. At first, I got in the car and drove anyway. I took the body's response to that willful behavior like a beating, but I told myself I had no choice. Then I couldn't do it anymore. I am now paying a driver to deliver me to class. I will teach online this fall.

I am learning and earning the freedom to participate with all of those unknown weavers of the national fabric in the cars beside me. All of those nameless drivers whom I must take on as colleagues as we bring to consciousness the cultural pains we've mostly carried in our bodies, carried in other people's bodies, isolated in the powerful weave of the *patria* that we claim is not us. But it is us. Even when we can't accelerate, can't control the flow of traffic, can't see what's coming next. We must do our best. To keep moving forward.

Right now, I am still moving in reverse. Take me back to the time when things felt possible. It is still there in my body. I have to believe this. Early childhood held possibility. Then came the years of trauma that I almost didn't survive. I've lost limbs and grown anew like the *axolotl*. My body knows the experience of surviving, then thriving. Right now, I have to trust that it's all there in my body. I feel like something two-dimensional these days. But I remember that I can reanimate, become 3-D with just the right turn, the right breath. I will open out like peace cranes from what seemed like flat paper. I just don't remember how.

Take me back to the time before, when I drove cross-country with no troubles. Sometimes sixteen hours in a day, back in the eighties when I lived in my truck and it was the Reagan administration. The AIDS epidemic. My friends were dying, and then I had a baby. Would they take my baby? I felt like my country was really truly trying to kill me. The car meant freedom then. The way dusk looked, coming over a ridge, coming over a bridge, a painted desert laid out around the road felt like a blanket welcoming me to peaceful slumber. You got this I'd say to myself. You got this. It all felt like freedom when I was moving. I can't move now, but I remember.

If the body keeps the score, then it's all in here. Somehow, I can go back by going forward. I can go forward by going back. The kahuna says that the ancestors and the generations to come all know what they're doing when they arrive in my body in the present moment. I can call them in.

It was all bravado back when I was still on the road during the first year of Trump. Somehow I could story myself through it. Maybe I still can, but not alone. The ghost of my father is with me. My mother and everyone else who voted for him, for what he represented, is with me. My son and his middle-class expectations, his whiteness and his anguish for all that his embodiment represents—he is with me. The foot that won't press the gas pedal now is the same foot that knew how to drive away from trouble before. We can't see what's just over the edge, what's ahead as the road curves. Life is a great mystery. That's for damned sure.

10.

BUTCH DYKES AND MACHO MEN

I hold masculinity in all of the gentle forms I can find.

Some people speculate about women like me—feminine gay women, lipstick lesbians, femme dykes. I've heard it all my life: maybe she's really straight. Maybe she's just fooling around with women. Maybe she would be with a man if only she weren't so ... damaged. We have been abused. We are fearful of men, and so we turn to women. I've felt the pity, the judgment, the scorn.

A person could get angry and want to fight about that sort of thing. I am gender: female, cisgender even, girly-normative. I like the erotic tension of masculine/feminine, so? A person could get defensive. I'm sure I've done my share of fighting and defending, but in good rhetorical style I have also considered this argument—not just to find the counterargument but also to find the logic in it. And, indeed, there's logic in it. I have been influenced by men's abuses. But then, I don't know anyone of any gender who has not been bruised, sometimes battered, by patriarchy, by the norms of masculinity.

I survived the incest of my parents' household and moved on to create a family free of incest. My son doesn't know the experience, nor does his father—at least so far as I am aware. I endured incest and other sexual assaults—as one-third or more of American women have endured incest, rape, and child molestation—sexual violence of some kind. Add in the men, the people of other genders, and we are not much of a minority. We are millions—and millions more still who've endured and brought to conscious reason the effects of patriarchy, the organization of a culture that, down to its small acts, supports the dominion of men over everyone else. In this climate, where the feminine is maligned, devalued, and sometimes torn stem from stern, it would be difficult to understand the existence of heterosexual women, were it not for sexual attraction and the desire for children. Indeed, how can heterosexual interactions be other than calculated—at least in small degree—because women most often stand to lose status and money via divorce. Whereas, men gain both. For all the popular culture stories and "I know this guy who lost everything" kind of talk, the statistics don't bear it out: women and children are driven into poverty by divorce every day. And in this climate, how can heterosexual relationships be felt as truly unfettered?

Neither are my relationships with women truly unfettered. The same social shackles that hold all others bind us. Indeed, I have often said that there is less homo and more hetero about my lovers and I. I am a femme dyke, attracted mostly to butch dykes; there are many ways to do attraction, but this is mine. We may be homosexual, but we are not homo-gendered. I do not date ladies. Could I not just be with a man?

I have been happy with male lovers, including trans men, and cismen. Though my passion burns brightest for masculine women, who knows where the fire originates? Part body, part culture is my guess. Most people live on the brittle boundaries of gender where everything seems based on biology, stable (though crumbling). I have always been soaked in the slippery center. None of my lovers were ladies; most weren't men. What are men? Women? Why do we persist? I have had good relationships with trans men, but do we get to say my comfort's quicker there because of my trans guy's "female" upbringing or a shared lesbian history (in most cases, not all)? Or do we assume that trans men live a deeper feminism somehow, muting the perceived perils of maleness? What do we assume, and who's the "we" assuming it?

My gay husband and I had a good sexual relationship for many years when our son was small. We were a nice gender-twisted couple; we met in the middle somehow: different bodies, overlapping genders. We had fun. We had love. What is attraction? Often the stories we tell about each other and ourselves inspire it—why else would a certain dress or haircut or shoes make the picture complete with one person, wrong with another? We don't rely on the scent of a certain musk to tell us "this is the one." We tell a subtler story that is revised often by appearances and actions and meaning.

Many heterosexual men cannot tell the story of how they participate in patriarchy—neither can many gay men nor many women of any romantic predilection. Maybe I could be attracted to more men—who could know? This is the world in which we live, where straight men are taught a certain hardness, and, while butch dykes and macho men often share interests and aesthetics, they are different. In the butches I've known, hardness yields differently. I know they remember the treatment of girlhood and that helps them understand my social position differently than most men ever would. If they find it in themselves to like the feminine in me, it's an informed liking, a real fondness, and a respect. Most butch dykes are not out to conquer femininity or protect it like a fragile prize. There can be something between us that is sweet and meaningful in a way that women in heterosexual unions only yearn toward. They rarely reach a true understanding of the things that make genders different but keep them kindred. We all grow from similar cells and DNA, and then we choose which differences are worth marking, which similarities we slip to the sidelines.

Things could be different. I could be attracted to men more often. Not all queer folks are the same. And maybe with the abolition of patriarchy—for it is only an idea, a practice—men would feel different attractions too. Gay and straight, men and women—everyone else—could feel different attractions. Perhaps we could speak more of this and not merely of my lack. If "being a girl" weren't the worst insult a man could give another, there could be a different love between men and women, men and men. The large numbers of men who call themselves straight but enjoy the occasional blow job from another man—the occasional or frequent sex with another man—might actually come to see their lovers differently. So much more could be allowed and shared if being "like a girl" were not such a sticky, contemptible identity.

My identity as a dyke sticks, I think, because of patriarchy. Without the shadow of the rules made to keep male privilege in place, we might all be different people. The only reason anyone feels the need to focus on the quandaries of my romances rather than their own is that I live outside of normal. And I am female: a certain locus of cultural victimization, pain, and damage. I am a gendered lightning rod for both pity and blame. Certain races, classes, abilities, and so on are also focal points for what a person lacks. The worst oppression is always the one happening to you right now.

This argument that I act and love from damage is not wholly wrong. And so do others whose loves and lives are seen as normal. There's no avoiding it—we are all damaged by a culture out of balance where rewards and meanings and sometimes even actions are hidden, even from ourselves.

This is a love letter to masculinity. I am deeply in love because along with my lack, I have fallen hard for possibility, for the way we can re-create wholeness using nothing more than our minds, our bodies, our words, our relationships, and our lives. I am in love with masculinity, and I am in love with possibility. This is a plea for all to join me in a good and gentle rhetorical interrogation of our gendered lives. What if, instead of just looking for the counterargument when an assertion wounds us, we seek the logic in it?

It makes sense that I hold masculinity in all of the comfortable forms I can find, just as all who love learn to do. How different would we be without the structures and sanctions we were given? We'll just have to try other ways to find out.

11.

NO GRAMMAR POLICE, BUT MAYBE A LEAGUE OF LANGUAGE ALTRUISTS

Sure. No one should be a jerk by telling people, unbidden, that they're saying something wrong or that they're using an incorrect part of speech or that their perfectly legible common-usage writing is misspelled. Not everyone has had the same level of education—and were you really confused anyway about what was meant when that person wrote "their" instead of "there"? Or "your" instead of "you're"?

People have used proper speech and proper grammar as a shield, as a way to feel better than someone else based on nothing but knowing the rules. Something like grammar can be just one of many ways to set up a hierarchy, rig the game, and declare oneself the winner.

Still, I think about George Orwell.

He figured out a few things about language and power and manipulation and stated them clearly fifty years ago. Namely, our use of language can guide our thinking, blunt our awareness, enliven our understanding. That's a lot, particularly when it's being used as a political tool. Just imagine what could happen if a group of people were having their thinking guided toward fascism, their awareness blunted so that myriad other options vanish. If this happens at the same time that fear is enlivened and hope diminished, imagine the damage a culture could sustain.

You don't need to imagine it; you're living it, so it's time to discuss the policing of grammar. As it turns out, language—how we use it, who's allowed to use it, and whose accounts have enough gravity to prompt action—is hugely important. At the same time, policing is a violent and often inappropriate way to maintain order.

Precision in language is important because it creates meaning, and, after all, language is really just standing in for ideas, for actions. Language is really just standing in for everything. The map is not the landscape, so why would burning the map harm the trees? It's not so much that we need to keep language intact through proper grammar as we need to keep meaning intact and legible across a wide range of experiences and ways of speaking and writing, expanding how the culture understands and what it finds important. (The Hawaiian word for "deconstruct," *makawalu*, literally means "eight eyes." Look with more than your own view.) The importance of precision in language is lost when its rules reinforce or create inequalities that can, in turn, humiliate and silence.

People get uncomfortable when language shifts, when meaning isn't immediately clear. It's not fun to think, *wow, I thought I understood, but I was wrong.* That feeling is instructive, though, particularly when the listener or reader is in a position of power. As a culture, we need to learn to expect that feeling and use it as an opportunity not only to expand understanding of marginalized views but also as a way to expand which views are deemed important. The multiplication of gender is a fine contemporary example.

I find it very difficult to use the plural when referring to individuals. A lot of people do, and there are likely a range of reasons why. My first difficulty is shared by many: I was taught and have practiced, as a writer and speaker, using *their* to refer to more than one person. In addition, I'm concerned with the lack of clarity that results from pluralizing an individual. I enjoy precise language unless ambiguity adds meaning. Aha. In this case, it does, so I'm catching up. People are claiming to embody more than one gender, and gender has previously been seen as a social binary. One *or* the other. No deviations.

Of course, there have always been deviations, and people are using the language both to illuminate that fact and to claim credibility for those who live outside the binary. The latter is at the root of a great deal of discomfort. Sometimes relationships are at stake when language is used wrongly, according to the desires of those being spoken of.

Moreover, the credibility and humanity of whole groups of people are at stake if we fail to take on their requests as credible. It's not so much that people find a name or pronoun change to be an insurmountable difficulty. The constant stumbling and forgetting of people's names and pronouns reveals the lack of respect for gender multiplicity.

For instance, when a woman marries and changes her last name to her husband's, people get it pretty quickly. It would be weird and disrespectful not to. Slip-ups can be treated with genuine good humor because the person who uses the old name is likely not seething behind a pleasant exterior and thinking, *marriage is so stupid. Why'd she do that? That name has nothing to do with her life and ancestry—why is she suddenly using it?*

Similarly, when a teacher is able to practice and properly pronounce the name Zofia Kowalczyk or Vasillis Papadapoulous but not Wang Xiu Ying Huang or Cuatemoc Vasquez, students receive a clear message about who is important and therefore credible and therefore valued. When I first began teaching at University of Hawaii, students with long Hawaiian names sometimes told me that I was the first white teacher they'd had pronounce their names correctly without mentioning the labor involved. The last part is important. Some teachers don't try, but, if they do, they want it known that they're making heroic effort. What would be the purpose of this, other than signaling charity?

The hesitation involved when being asked to call someone John instead of Mary has nothing to do with linguistic effort but with the credibility of the request. It's useful for each of us, when uncomfortable, to consider why. I understand why a person would want to be referred to as plural. In fact, we are all a collection of multiplicities, multiple sites and citations. Our very ability to use language in interesting ways relies on the palimpsest of human culture and expression. I understand why a person would find "he" or "she" limiting, why a person would want to go by "they" instead. And sometimes the plural and the singular become a conundrum that leads to the passive voice—which can obscure who, exactly, is doing what—or other oddly contorted language couplings that avoid the use of pronouns. All of these are useful things to consider.

In some ways, avoiding certain words leads to creativity—as when one is using a newly acquired language and must simply talk around words one doesn't know. But this game can also become political, speaking around what is known to offend, rather than stating things plainly. For instance, we rarely discuss racial segregation in schooling in the United States these days, though it's worsened, in some ways, since we declared it legally solved in 1954. We use words like "diversity" and "community schooling" to avoid even acknowledging how racially segregated housing and schooling have constructed our everyday lives.

It isn't that the passive voice is never useful. Sometimes one wants to highlight a subject in the sentence that normally would not be the subject, even if that subject is being *done to*. It's important that we can do that, that we can draw attention to things and to people that normally are not the subject by rearranging the way the sentence is structured. Often times, however, the passive voice causes the person doing the action to be left out in a significant way. The passive voice becomes a way to conceal who is actually doing things, and when we want those parties to stop doing those things it becomes very important that we name them. For instance, it's almost never true, at least not completely true, that twenty women were raped. To say it that way: "twenty women were raped last week" sounds as though the raping happened by ethereal forces. It's more important to focus on who did the raping, that is, to be able to say plainly that five or eight or twenty men raped twenty women. Or maybe the rapists were women or dogs or teenagers or goats; I don't want to assume. Emphatically, I don't want to assume. I want to say specifically what I know, and I want other women to do the same, especially if they have been raped by someone specific, which people almost always are.

Similarly, it's almost never wholly true, in a war, that five villages burned to the ground. I want to know who did the burning. I want to know who was left without a home. I want detail and nuance in those stories so that we can each decide what to do so that it does not happen again. Burned villages, after all, and rapes, are painful and should not be something simply consumed in news stories as though they are unconnected to human lives. Once it's clear exactly what is happening, attention can be drawn to the fact that certain problems prompt remedy and others, such as women being raped or certain people losing their homes, prompt eye-rolling and shrugs. Our ability to devalue certain people—indeed, to realize that we devalue them—is damaged by imprecise language.

Obfuscations of language, using passive constructions, are particularly rampant in areas where people don't wish to be questioned, as in politics and academia. That's the purpose of an academic argument, after all: to close all the exits and prove something in an unassailable way. And then the game is on, where other academics try to assail the argument and win, if only on technicalities of language and meaning and the construction of an argument, which paradoxically (see above) may be very important indeed. I try to help the graduate students in the program where I teach understand that despite their glee in having just learned to close the exits in an argument or to assail a closed argument, neither skill is very good at enhancing meaning. In most settings, being cleverly critical doesn't make you respectable; it makes you an asshole.

The bad thing about people appointing themselves as grammar police is not that grammar is unimportant but that policing is a violent way of creating order. One party is empowered to give either help or punishment. The other party takes it, passively. I'd like to see a league of grammar altruists, like a volunteer fire service in which a good number of community members participate for everyone's benefit. A league of altruists can be available when needed, rest when not needed, and it's okay that some have a level of skill and kindness that not everyone possesses. I'd like to see something like that rather than eye-rolling enforcement of a set of rules by which some people are judged the winners in an invisible game of worthiness. Then more, ever more, are judged the losers. Maybe we can keep everyone safe and happy in their manifold expressions and still not let the village burn down.

In George Orwell's essay "Politics and the English Language," he pointed out how ready-made words and phrases come so easily into our minds and into our lives, making us easier to control. Quite simply, he advocated "picking words for their meaning and inventing images in order to make the meaning clearer."

It is not nice to put someone else down for their lack of understanding of language, but it's downright damaging to ignore that we are easily manipulated by those who use language more skillfully than we do. Luckily, these are not the only two choices—not nearly the only two. We dare not forget that language is a tool that can control as well as inform as well as heal and enlighten. At the very same time that I love Orwell's assertions about clarity, it's misguided to think that language can ever declare clear, vivid, and totally shared meaning. Many live in interstitial meaning-spaces where their forms of expression are devalued. Being prompted toward another person's idea of clarity can feel abusive. And that doesn't make clarity any less important. Adrienne Rich makes daily sense for many: "This is the oppressor's language, yet I need it to talk to you."

Language is always mirroring and creating culture. This simultaneous mirroring and creating make it all the more important that deviations from the rules of language exist. And how they exist matters. Every deviation from a norm carries meaning—more accurately, meanings. Those who know how language currently functions help shed light on those meanings. When individuals are deviating involuntarily from standard usage, they are far more likely to be labeled as deviant themselves, or deficient or perhaps even stupid. And these designations serve no one but an elite minority who benefit from current power structures. Artful deviations, however, shine a light through the cracks in this system of conformity and reward. Intentional and creative deviations are very useful, and the people who make them can go a long way toward multiplying and then amplifying the compassionate, radical, and multifarious meanings endemic to human expression.

As a person with a fairly large vocabulary, I acknowledge that I have sometimes been one of those people who tried to use language as a shield, to use language to bolster my own credibility, which is always done at someone else's expense. I don't think it was a bad choice during the moments that I was in danger of dismissal. More than once, someone looked at me, looked at my body, and judged me less-than on my supposed failings. Growing into adolescence with a fat fertility-symbol-shaped body, being seen as not quite white enough—there was a lot of less-making going on. I innovated around those circumstances in order to be understood and loved. Language was but one of the tools I used for stigma management.

I hope I was not the type of grammar police who used language like a weapon against others. But I know I may have been in my youth and still might be on occasion now. Anyone among us who puts on the uniform of policing—whether for noble or selfish aims—is capable of doing others harm.

In part, I developed a large vocabulary because I was in an upper-middle-class milieu where adults expected children to learn well and move on to college. I had access to literature and a higher quality of public education than most. I also became intimate with language as an escape during a time when my mind needed something to do to distract from my body. Memorizing passages of British literature was a big part of how I passed the time while my stepfather sexually abused me. When he called me savage, in part to excuse those acts, I researched and read to see where my experiences and appearance fit with that word and with others who'd heard that word used against them. Some of this was my initiative; some was opportunity. It's not that I loved British literature specifically or had access to the kind of knowledge about immigration, slavery, colonization, and genocide that I would later in my life, but I found solace in language. I lived in the type of household—that is to say, an American household preparing a child for a college education—in which British and American literature were the only things available.

A league of grammar altruists, rather than a force of grammar police, might be helpful, with the aim of addressing the damage that unclear and manipulative language can cause. It's always possible to wield one's knowledge as a tool or a weapon. I am thinking of the similarly contentious relationship that many have with manners in social settings. Ideally having "good manners" is a way to habituate kindness even when there are other things on one's mind. It is a way to ease social interactions so that no one feels badly or out of place in any setting. Manners can be used to welcome those who might not otherwise feel invited, and, of course, they can be used to exclude.

Ideally good manners facilitate civil interaction. The paradox is that manners are used as protocols to decide who is an insider and who is an outsider. They are used to enforce a hierarchy of worth where none truly exists among an assembled group. They are used to bully and belittle, just as the rules of grammar can be used to exclude. The wielding of both manners and grammar depends on the intent and disposition of the individual; are they for altruistic aims or to bolster ego or gain? The altruists must be nimble, flexible.

Just as when people police other's manners they become guilty of poor manners themselves, so too when people police grammar they are drawing attention away from the truly important aspects of language which are meaning, communication, and connection. At their worst, politeness and manners conceal what should be discussed. They keep people two-faced and willing to maintain a façade of niceness to enforce obedience rather than actually discussing important matters. Indeed the policing of anyone keeps the focus on order and conformity and rule-following rather than on creativity, innovation, kindness, and the sort of orderliness that allows people to develop their talents fearlessly and give their gifts well.

Unfortunately, people with nefarious agendas will harm others through language whether or not those others ever learn to listen and understand carefully, whether or not those others ever learn to use the tools of language well themselves. If Orwell was naive to assume a direct dialectical relationship between thought and language, at least he was practical about it. Relational, postmodernist thinking doesn't keep the cake from being delicious, the sea from being wet, and the handcuffs from restraining, at least on most days of the week.

Using the wrong spelling of "their" will not obscure meaning in a small interaction. That kind of inattentiveness with language can nonetheless lead to distractions with dire consequences. When our vocabularies and grammars are limited, in a time when other forms of creative expression are also blunted and conformity is rewarded, we lose stories, perspectives, and solutions.

How would it look to encourage a love of expression and relationship? That's what June Jordan was doing by infusing her poetry with specific everyday language that illuminated care and consequences. Because, goodness knows, language isn't the only game around, and image production as communication has every problem inherent in language and then some. How would it look to encourage people, not to shame one another based on what they don't know or how they look or what kind of ideas they're expressing? How would it look for altruistic language lovers to help each other develop more vibrant forms of expression and to help even those who are not interested in language expression to become more vibrant listeners, readers, and creators in their own media? How would it be for individuals focused on the love of expression and the diverse ways humans manifest in order to create forms of expression that move beyond language in everyday communication? That's the kind of "learning to be clear" that would be useful to a civil society. One in which we have the good manners not to bully one another because of diverse expressions. In answering these questions, we may come closer to a kind and just society that does not tolerate the suppression of any of its perspectives.

12.

HOW WE COME TO DO IT
TO EACH OTHER

I.

Sure, it's horrible. It's not like I don't know. It's been done to me too. I am telling myself it could be worse. At least I'm not mean about it; at least I'm giving it thoughtful consideration. I know what this humiliation is like. I'm not going to make her look at me. I am reasoning with myself as I lower my body onto hers.

My mind acknowledges age: I am older. Of course, I am older and know what to do, what has to be done. I acknowledge the tragedy of skin color. She seems to be Black, and I seem to be white. See how I maneuver language into the tight spaces of my mind as I do it? This is no theoretical equation. I'm not just talking about socialization, like I do all day, about how we learned to disdain certain people and so we do it even if we are also those people. This is flesh on flesh.

Nothing I acknowledge makes me stop doing it.

I am pushing against her flesh, saying I'm sorry, and she has turned away from me slightly, biting her lip. It seems like it takes forever. At one point she whispers, "Just do it." She wants me to stop being so timid and get it over with. And I am doing it. Her body is warm against me, and of course the heat is rising in mine as well. This must be how some rapists think as they forge ahead. Justify. Acknowledge the details, and then do it anyway. Make excuses. At least I don't like it. See there, I did it again.

This must be how some rapists take the social position that has been given to them and act as though they are not the ones doing what they are doing even though flesh against flesh is undeniable. Fear and pain in the eyes of the other is undeniable. "Just do it" resignation is tragic. In war, when rape is a tool, ordered, certainly, this is what it must be like. Just do it. But also at parties, drunk girl lying in an upstairs bedroom. Your teammates in the hallway saying, "G'on man, it's your turn." Your teammates. Is that what it's like? She's stopped being "that girl at school" and is now something to be moved through toward a social destination that seems more important than ... assault.

I don't know whether this analogy has gone too far. How could I know how far it should go? When I realize that my training to do this has included having it done to me? Damage enables us to damage others and let it feel familiar, something we just survive, like before. Forget that we are carrying the brokenness forward. Forget. Holy shit. I mean really. Holy shit.

II.

Of course I noticed her in the security line. A tall fat woman with style! Who's not going to notice her? My first thoughts were about the long, nubbly fabric vest she was wearing. I would *so* wear that vest! Great color against her dark skin, hangs nice over the comfy pants. Big hair is fab on her. She has the big soft dreadlock-like hair extensions in three contrasting colors hanging well down her back, pulled up tall on top. I mean, I love tall hair and big earrings. She's tall anyway—maybe 6'3; I love the audacity of more height. She looks so young to have figured out such style in such a large body. I am eyeing the boots too. She has thinner calves than mine, and those boots look like cheap ones. Payless makes some wider calf styles now, I recall. Not in my day. I feel a bit smug about having figured out some style as a young person with fewer ready-made resources. She's bigger than me, taller by a few inches for sure. Our bodies are differently shaped, but this woman has a fashion sense with which I felt kindred. She sat next to me in the waiting lounge on the long bench where we could both comfortably chat and we traded compliments.

She asked me questions about her boarding pass and her next connection, and then she had a little video conversation on her phone with her boyfriend. I overheard enough to know it was her boyfriend. He would miss her while she was away from New York in Montana. He was going to miss her more than she'd miss him, by the sound of it.

I travel by air so often that I'm actually surprised this hasn't happened to me before. Usually I'm just thinking about how to navigate being the seatmate others dread or fear. The fat passenger is like the crying baby or the kicking toddler. People are entitled to hate me the moment they see me, so here's what I do. I'm nice. I act entitled to be there. I remain calm. I figure these are a public service as much as they are good for me to assert my own right to air travel. This is what I think about as I walk up that aisle to find my seat.

How strange that it never occurred to me that *this* could happen. Of course it could happen. I'm never the only fat person on a flight. What if two of us are sitting together?

I like to wait until boarding is nearly complete so I don't spend any more time on the plane than needed. Mine was the only empty seat by the time I got on. Oh no. It's her.

The first thing I feel is panic. They're going to put one of us off this plane if I don't play this right. I am the one standing in the aisle, not able to take a seat. It might be me. But I am also the middle-aged white lady with a long history in this airline's frequent flier program, and she is the young, shamed-nearly-to-invisibility Black woman who can't buckle her seat belt. I can't lose either one of us. I have to do something that protects both of us.

I can't bear to be the one who makes her so vividly seen, if there's conflict with flight attendants. It might be either one of us who is asked to leave. My mind starts to immediately manage the situation. I look around the aircraft, assess the geography, discern the allies, decide who to be and what to say, if anything. No, that's not what happens first. First I see her, and my heart clenches with compassion and anguish at how she looks at me, defeated.

III.

Some people have less body contact during sex than she and I had on that flight. That's how I started thinking about the rape analogy.

That and the shame. The flavor of it was so familiar coming off of her body. I'msorryI'msorryI'msorry. The flavor of it was so familiar coming off of my body. I was just doing what had to be done, and I knew the doing was possible.

I seriously had to strategize my entry into that seat. I wasn't sure we could fit at all. Her body already did not allow for the seat divider to be put down and it was a small two-seat row. The size of the seats and how the plane curves on the window side vary by aircraft. She could only push herself so far against the wall. Still standing in the aisle, I asked the flight attendant for a seat belt extender. I asked my seatmate if she wanted one too, before the attendant reached us, but she shook her head and looked at me as if to say, "god, please don't. one more thing. no." I attached it before lowering myself into the space. I knew I'd be up on one hip, turned toward her because turning away would've put too much of me in the aisle for anyone to pass, let alone the cart, later. I would need to press against her with some force to even get my body wedged into the space available.

Let me stop using the conditional future verb tense in this description, which is easier because it places me in another more analytic moment than the one I mean to describe.

I am shifting onto one foot to turn my body toward her and wedge my hip down onto the seat. This is causing the top of my body to press into the side of her body. She is shifting to move away from me, and for a moment I do the reflexive thing and stop pushing. She is moving away, and I am pursuing with my own body, and I stop for a moment because this does not feel right to be forcing my body onto a stranger's body. That's when she whispers, resigned, "Just do it." She is looking away from me, biting her lip. I am afraid she will cry. I am afraid I will cry. Her body is warm, and I can feel that there are three rolls of flesh between her hip and armpit. Her arm, the one closest to me, is raised so that I can get closer. She is also up on one hip as much as possible in her pinned-to-the-window position. In order to speed this up, I make one final push and shimmy around to buckle my extended seat belt. Once I'm in, my head is no longer on her shoulder, as it was in that push. The flesh of my behind is pushed painfully against the outer edge of the seat. I need only endure it until the fasten seat belts sign is off, I tell myself. I will be marked, sore for days, from the containment.

IV.

She sat totally still and compressed for 150 minutes. I stood for most of the flight, in the aisle next to my seat, and I didn't see her relax her arms once. If there were people on this flight laughing at our pain, or ridiculing us with their eyes or gestures or words, I didn't see it. I could not see the other passengers at all. I was so angry for her pain. More so than I could be for my own in similar situations. This delightful young woman with the great hair, the cute outfit, the boyfriend missing her from New York probably didn't think she was getting on the plane to be humiliated by me today.

Or am I not the one who humiliated her? Is it the airline? Is it a culture that tells the airline it's okay to do this, to treat bodies as though they are similar enough that no accommodations need be made for size differences. Is it the culture that says fat people deserve so much humiliation that all of this can happen in public, in full view of others, and it's totally normal? In any case, my body was the instrument of her pain and humiliation. I could've resisted, refused. I was already in the process of doing "what needed to be done" before I even considered resistance.

And who are the flight attendants in this unfolding drama? It was exceedingly clear when I asked for a seatbelt extender that I was next to a person who was larger than me and that she would need an extender too in order to comply with the lighted symbols. It was as though my seatmate was invisible to the flight attendant, even as she was glaringly obvious because of her size. The flight attendant was standing right there, interacting with me as though the other passenger did not exist. My seatmate even had her bag on her lap, wedged between her body and the seatback in front of her. There was no way she could've bent forward to stow it beneath the seat. I expected the flight attendant to snatch it into an overhead bin, but no, not even that.

I've seen seatbelt-refusers before. Some passengers don't fit in the seatbelt, don't bring a seatbelt extender, don't ask for one, and are openly visible not wearing the seatbelt, and flight attendants don't even look their way. I had an extended conversation with a friendly flight attendant about this matter and she said, "I personally try to be accommodating and discreet [about seat belt extenders]. Not all flight attendants are, and I'm sorry for that. We can only request passengers wear a seatbelt. If they choose not to, they put themselves and other passengers at risk for injury... You can't force or shame someone into wearing their seatbelt."

Flight attendants are humans constrained by social convention as well. To look at and interact with fat people is to humiliate them. Ignoring them is benevolent—and also saves the speaker discomfort. Some flight attendants feel the need to intervene to take fat people off of planes, others look away from that which is uncomfortable. They are managing their workplace comfort as we all do, with little guidance from their employers, it seems.

At the end of the day, after I have cried privately about this scene and relived the feeling of her frightened flesh against me far too many times, what I am left with is the responsibility for having violated her. I am left with the weight of my own past violations when someone else felt they were just doing what needed to be done. I am left with the intergenerational nature of fat bodies being abused and how those with just a little more privilege than others are recruited as overseers, as mascots for oppression, as organizers. I am a little smaller than she and older, and I know how the airline system works. I know that no smaller person would've voluntarily taken either of us as a seatmate so that we could all sit down during the flight. In a pinch, I did the airline industry's job for them by violating someone rather than disrupting the smooth operation of their workday. We were in a pinch, and the company, the industry, the culture put us there. I probably did the thing she most wanted me to do too, though I can't say for sure. Chances are, either one of us being put off the plane would've been hard for her too.

I can remember feeling as she looked, in the airport, when I was a young person. Ready to disappear yet determined to live a full life, show some fashion sense, travel. I put up a force field around my body that said "You may not talk to me about this body unless it is to discuss how hot I am or how great it is that I can do two aerobics classes back to back and still bike home. Do you understand?!"

Mostly, that worked. Strangers and loved ones will collude with stigma management as long as you have other laudable traits to offer. Most of the time. But then there are social circumstances that call attention to the body, and people feel entitled to comment or manage us in more overt ways than expected. Usually, this has to do with navigation of prescribed space. Usually, a prescribed space on which someone stands to profit if we remain "managed." Make no mistake. These moments—participating in them, or witnessing them silently as every person on that plane did—prepare us for and normalize other moments of looking away. People living on the streets in large numbers, homeless children, were not a tolerable sight when I was young, and then, in the 1980s, they became so. Children taken from their parents and locked up without care have become part of the cultural landscape in the past few years. I currently see no end to what evils a culture will tolerate. I like to think I know what I will tolerate, but I don't know. I cannot now know.

I can say this: "It's happened before and it'll probably happen again." I could be seated next to someone fatter than me on a flight. What will I do when that happens? I can't say. I will again use my discernment. I may even get off the plane myself rather than take the oppressor role again. It probably depends on how much income I stand to lose by doing so, if I fail to show up for a job by missing the plane. That's the bottom line. It'll depend on how much I have to lose and my relationship to that loss.

As we got off the plane, I gave her as much psychic love and comfort as I could. I wished her well for the next flight and offered my name. She only spoke hers in a whisper.

13.

FAT PEDAGOGY IN THE YOGA CLASS

The significant artifact

This is a story about what it means to allow the body to be seen. To be seen in movement, to be seen in pleasure, to be seen as the model for the physical pose for alignment, for peace. It's about beauty and acceptance as tools for teaching others, consciously wielded and constantly part of unconscious exploration. It's about vulnerability, persistence, and strength. In addition to *talking* to help bring yoga students into the experience of the body, teachers allow them to witness our *experience* of being in our own bodies. During teaching, we are each internal subjects, in addition to being seen by students. We can never fully understand what we're offering, except through contemplation of our experience and of the comments and nonverbal responses we receive from others. We model presence and confidence and vulnerability. Indeed, we offer a holistic experience of being as a model. I am a fat woman—among many other identities—and therefore I offer a fat pedagogy, whether or not I ever articulate it in the yoga studio.

The body is the significant artifact.

Artifact, *noun*

1. *any object made by human beings, especially with a view to subsequent use.*

2. *a handmade object, as a tool, or the remains of one, as a shard of pottery, characteristic of an earlier time or cultural stage, especially such an object found at an archaeological excavation.*

3. *any mass-produced, usually inexpensive object reflecting contemporary society or popular culture*

The body itself may be a different kind of noun, an organic form. But what we make of bodies socially—the ways in which we socially construct the meaning of bodies—becomes the artifact. We are performative creatures; our bodies are both product and process, and our ways of being influence others. When my fat body teaches yoga, the expectation of what media-culture has taught us that fat bodies can and should do (things like sitting, eating, crying, rolling over, and being sick, sad, and dying) is disturbed by the fact of my body moving and speaking in the yoga teacher role. The resulting dissonance becomes part of the teaching space I hold for students. Even if we never speak of it (though sometimes we do), my body is enacting fat pedagogy.

Every yoga teacher comes to terms with what it means to be seen. And that's no small matter, for women in particular. Already positioned as "the weaker sex," women often reach an unassailable pinnacle of whatever form of fitness they practice before they allow the body to be seen. As sociologist Erving Goffman explained back in the 1950s, we manage identity using a variety of artful means. We manage our identities to find basic comfort, to maximize privilege, and to minimize oppression. The body is always teaching, and even more so in classes, like yoga, where the body is demonstrating form. Even when teaching topics, like sociology, that ostensibly involve only the minds of students and teachers, my body is teaching. People think they can overlook my body, but it's never true. I am still providing an example of how varying vehicles can carry the mind. As a yoga teacher, I am providing an example of how varying vehicles can show asana. My "performances" of self always involve the body as significant artifact. And students manage the dissonance using linguistic constructions like this: She's fat but she's brilliant. She's fat but she's graceful. She's fat but she's beautiful. The fat body remains the significant artifact because it's so powerfully salient to every aspect of social life for women. We are socialized to live in constant relationship to fat—either being fat, avoiding being fat, or being glad we're not fat. No matter what I do, so long as it doesn't conform to the preset cultural standards for fat bodies—sloth, gluttony, dull-mindedness, disease, and death—there will always be a "but."

Through my work as a writer, storyteller, and performer, I've learned about the significance of embodied storytelling. My embodiments are varied, of course—I speak from a fat body, a queer body, a female body, a mixed-race-white-privileged body, et cetera. I started touring my first solo theatre show in 1998, titled *The Butch-Femme Chronicles: Discussions with Women Who Are Not Like Me (and Some Who Are)*. I thought the success of that show derived from how audiences were engaging with the stories and poems I'd written. Over time, I realized that my onstage presence was also an important element of the show's success. It's not just that I was telling stories about lesbian lives; I was an actual lesbian, on stage for ninety minutes, available for viewing. This may sound strange nowadays, but remember that the visibility of gay and lesbian people who actually talk about being gay and lesbian has exploded in the last decade. I started performing before Ellen DeGeneres "came out" on television. I was a breathing, moving artifact, animating stories that offered emotion, detail, and analysis.

Maya Maor's "Becoming the Subject of Your Own Story: Creating Fat Positive Representations" discusses the "politics of the familiar and the ordinary" in an analysis of my performance work. I bring to life, onstage, the ambiguity and complexity of a stigmatized appearance. Maor explores the ways in which my fat embodiment is "ambiguous," along with how the intersections of my various identities complicate the external gaze. The ways in which students are both disturbed and comforted by complexity are similar when I teach yoga.

Really think this through: my body type is normally seen as a cautionary tale, not as a site of peace and practice and beauty, action, and joy. My fat body is more readily pictured on a sofa, or, if working, behind a desk. If I ask you to picture an American woman, nearly fifty years old, weighing over three hundred pounds, you are not likely to picture her in a range of pursuits. You are not likely to say, "well, I need more information than that to be able to picture her. What does she like to do?" She is not assumed to like to do anything (except, maybe, eat). She is static, and it pains you to move her, just as much as you imagine it pains her to move.

The predetermined ontology of the body is already in play when one considers the fat body. And I disrupt it directly by being physical in many specific settings, manners, and pursuits. I also reinforce it at times. I allow myself to be seen in my limitations and in the modifications I take that less bulky bodies do not need to take (at least not for the sake of navigating fat). I cannot escape these cultural strictures, can't live outside of the culture. I can, however, prompt a somewhat different functioning of those strictures through compliance and disruption, just as when people interrupt other forms of violence, damage, and oppression by living into them with specific bodies that defy full regulation.

There comes to be a pedagogy that derives from the ontology of bodies—whether they are super-fit or soft and motherly, or fat or old or disabled or beautiful, or any combination of these. Whether consciously or not, we each enact a pedagogy of embodiment in addition to whatever other approaches we take to teaching. It's just that slender bodies are rendered "neutral" in the yoga studio, much as all privileged identities become invisible as social defaults of normality. No one's body is neutral; we are each enacting a pedagogy of form. My fat pedagogy is as conscious as I can make it. I explore it in the hopes that a) others' embodied paradigms and pedagogies become more visible and so that b) it becomes easier to respect the wisdom and necessity of diverse bodily paradigms and pedagogies.

Allowing the Body to Be Seen

"Beauty isn't all about just nice, loveliness-like. Beauty is about more rounded, substantial becoming. And I think when we cross a new threshold, that if we cross it worthily, what we do is we heal the patterns of repletion that were in us that had us caught somewhere. And in our crossing, then we cross into new ground where we don't just repeat what we've been through in the last place we were. So I think beauty in that sense is about an emerging fullness, a greater

sense of grace and elegance, a deeper sense of depth and also a kind of
homecoming for the enriched memory of your unfolding life."

—John O'Donohue, "The Inner Landscape of Beauty"

People often talk about yoga practice as having liberated them from
something they couldn't name. Yoga is more than fitness, yet hatha
yoga is rooted in movement of the breath and body. People often speak
of yoga as having freed them and allowed them to see more beauty
in themselves and in others. That's why the poet John O'Donohue's
thoughts on beauty come to mind as I consider the process of allowing
the body to be seen. It is indeed a process. I am always the artifact, and
the unfolding, as I occupy the teacher's mat. Our socially constructed
views on body shame and worthiness are indeed a threshold that must
be crossed if we are to move toward peace and acceptance.

I choose how I allow my body to be seen. So do you. We are always
living two lives: one as the subject of our own stories, in which we make
meaning of who we are, what we do and say. This life-as-subject is still
a socially mitigated life, and it also contains an internal flair and flavor.
It contains choice. We dress or undress, adorn or simplify, follow or
reject cultural standards for appearance, show up in a range of settings,
or remain in private space only. These are our choices. The second life is
as the object of external interpretations. Those interpretations can bring
privilege or pain, include or exclude us in specific settings, and sometimes limit how we are able to receive help or remain part of a community. When external interpretations sanction us, the results can be trivial
or deadly. This is no game. I choose how I allow my body to be seen,
and, when I can stay conscious about it, I choose when and how I allow
others' interpretations to affect me.

I am continually crossing a threshold within myself regarding social interpretations, expectations, privileges, and the possibility
for oppression. Sure, in the studio where I teach, I have a reasonable
amount of comfort. I have the credibility of simply occupying the
teacher role. Athletic credibility also assists the fat body in finding

comfort. I had that through my thirties and into my early forties—the credibility of what people called "an impressive practice." That's waning for me, though a trained eye can often see a long-term yoga practice in my body. I notice that when I'm a student in other studios, my emotional stability can waver depending on how welcome I feel, how out of place I feel. This is true even though I also teach. Indeed, after decades of nearly always being the fattest participant in the yoga studio, in the gym, or on the hiking trail, my own visibility can still exhaust me. This visibility in the student role is complex. Jeannine Gailey explores this complexity in her book *The Hyper(in)visible Fat Woman,* in which she investigates individual perceptions and social expectations. "Hyper(in) visibility" is the seemingly paradoxical social position of being paid exceptional attention—often negative, sanctioning attention—while simultaneously being erased. As a student, I'm often expected to fend for myself when it comes to posture modifications, and, still, I can feel scrutinized by the teacher and other students. I recall once, during my first class with a particular teacher, being told I wasn't capable of downward dog and should simply take a resting pose. Even as I explained that I had practiced downward dog daily for decades, the teacher's simultaneous scrutiny and erasure of my practice prevailed throughout the class.

I am aware that I choose to cross the threshold of exhaustion into comfort and peace not only for myself but for others as well. It's helpful when I remember that I disturb stereotypes for the common good as well as for my own sake. Being slender or fit or young or hegemonically beautiful does not exempt one from the physical and emotional trauma of body tyranny and expectations of conformity. Some of us are just more able to see it, all around us. I practice peace and pleasure in a fat, aging, queer, female body for the good of all. And I do so publicly. In the teacher role, my "hyper(in)visibility" and I become fully visible. Students are supposed to look at my body and consider its positions.

My body is vulnerable to social interpretations, and in being vulnerable I draw subtle attention to everyone's vulnerability. All bodies experience social critique—and some are more vulnerable to sanction or actual injury than others. Female bodies more than men's, people of color more than white bodies, genderqueer bodies more than cisgender bodies, fat bodies more than thin ones, to name a few. Can the vulnerable body be powerful?

As a yoga teacher, I allow my body to be seen in movement, to be seen in pleasure, to be seen as the model—not of a laudable body type but of specific movements, joint rotations, muscular effort, states of being. Allowing my body's limitations to be seen by saying things like "this doesn't work on my body, but you may be able to…" can be powerful for students who can't take every "further" modification suggested. I specifically tell students not to take every option suggested. Accept when "it's not your pose." Accept the modification. You are not invited to every party. Neither am I. We're going to be fine sometimes staying home or going to another party. And too, sometimes it's great to accept an invitation you wouldn't normally consider. The pose is like a party—a choice, something to enjoy, perhaps a challenge, but not an expectation, a way to judge human worth.

I also allow my body to be in community. I participate in the creation of the community I occupy. I teach in a retreat center where large, mixed-level classes are the norm. We also offer private and small group classes. My students include athletes and fitness beginners, yoga teachers and those who've never practiced before. The people who come through are mostly young to middle-aged and fairly active and they are also fat, thin, young, old, able, and disabled. I help people focus on the specifics of doing asana safely, to notice pleasure in the body, the information in the body. I am teaching specific people, not just teaching yoga asanas. We use props and modifications in every class.

When I reveal my vulnerability, along with the steadiness of my practice, I'm offering the possibility of finding strength and solid ground within a vulnerable position. I am vulnerable to cultural damage because of what my culture sometimes calls a failed body, a defective body, a disabled body. Crossing the threshold from damaged to vulnerable can create its own sort of power. My social position (related to body stigma) is not likely to change much in my lifetime. Indeed, it's likely to intensify with age. The fact is, if we're lucky enough to live long lives, we'll all be stigmatized by age and declining ability. I often remind students that there are good reasons why we practice corpse pose at the end of every class. That's where we're all heading, after all, and so learning acceptance and peace in the body now is relevant for all. I can't control how others see me, and I can influence community. I can develop a solid yet malleable understanding of myself. Often, students report that this modeling allows them to rest their own pursuit of perfection—not just in the postures but also in various aspects of life. All of that is part of my fat pedagogy.

Yoga Is for the Body You Have Today: A Pedagogy of Omission

I often say some version of this when I teach hatha classes: "Yoga is for the body you have today, not the body you had yesterday or last year or fifteen years ago. Not the one you will have tomorrow or next week or next year after you've practiced every day, or after you've learned to love yourself, or after you've given up ice-cream." There are endless humorous and poignant comments I can squeeze from examples that convey this truth: now is all we have. No matter how the mind negotiates and avoids this fact, now is all we have. If you want to be present, then accepting exactly this body is part of that. If you place value on ahimsa, on stilling the waves of the mind so that you can rest in true consciousness, the body is part of that. We are not separable from our bodies during hatha yoga (arguably not at any other time before death). Yet how often do people conditionally accept their bodies, all while claiming to be present?

The body from which I speak matters when I say "This is the only body you have. Yoga is for this body. Accept this body." I know that some students are wondering how I can mean that, while other students are thinking, wow, I think she really means she accepts her body. Similarly, when a slender teacher or a visibly muscular teacher says such things, the student may think, wow, look how clear-thinking, liberated, and advanced she is. Or conversely, sheesh, of course she can love and accept herself; look at those abs. We are never speaking—or thinking—from the mind alone. The body is involved.

In my classes, I talk more about the body than about philosophy. I include some of the yoga sutras and chants and stories about Hindu mythology, but minimally. According to my eclectic training (including Iyengar-style teaching) I talk more about alignment than affirmations. I draw attention to bodies that show clear examples of good posture, including my own, and I look for a range of body types to use as examples when I do this. Any body can potentially be a clear example of positioning, effort, variations on the pose. A huge part of pedagogy lies in what we choose to exclude in each sixty-, seventy-five-, or ninety-minute class. So much of popular culture can be replicated in spaces like yoga studios, or we can consciously choose to omit the aspects that are incongruent with the yoga sutras, the namas, and the niyamas. We each bring our sum of self, our opinions (even subtly conveyed in the way we hold our bodies, glance, dress, etc.). No one is teaching "pure" yoga. I don't believe such a thing exists. All ideologies must become practical when we bring them into our bodies, our communities. I also practice the feminism of this body, the anarchism of this body. As the body learns to rest into itself, as it changes with time, the way it lives into ideology evolves. We combine lineage, training, and innovation. Thus has yoga progressed from its beginning into the present day.

I often attend classes that include contemplations, affirmations, and I'm not against them. Indeed, "Yoga is for the body you have today" is an affirmation of sorts. I specifically don't use affirmations that reference the appearance of the body, outside of positioning in the asana. The kundalini teacher in a class I recently attended said, "If you want to get ripped abs, keep practicing breath of fire!" He seemed to truly believe that the appearance of his abs originated in breath of fire. Consider how absurd it would be for me to point to my fat arms and say, "this is the result of twenty-five years practicing plank pose!" I'm very careful about language and causation, though many teachers link appearance and practice without care.

In another example, my yoga teacher friend used to routinely say, "Come into your body and feel gratitude. You have two arms, two legs, your sight and hearing!" I asked him once if he really meant that's why we should be grateful. Conversely, did he mean that blind students or amputees could not experience gratitude in a yoga practice. He saw my point. This type of verbal encouragement—in part because yoga is routinely practiced by a relatively privileged group in the United States—is endemic to studio banter.

We have to work at awareness, phrasing, and word choice. For instance, I exclude comments about bodies that are often seen as laudable, unless it's about the pose. "Let's see what's going well in this trikonasana!" I might say. Though it's sometimes tempting—especially when someone is well-dressed, or particularly graceful in that lithe, willowy way we're taught to admire, I don't comment on beauty, fitness, style, et cetera. We may indeed share an ideal image of these things— but I don't choose to reinforce that association. I prefer to point out how everyone can enjoy the experience of the body. The appearance of the body is simply not of concern, unless it's about posture and modification.

The first teacher with whom I learned to teach, Sherri Jones, was an Iyengar-style instructor. She mentored me, apprentice-style, during a span of two years, in which time I assisted in classes she taught and subbed for classes when she was away. My learning with her included fewer sessions in which she taught me to teach and more opportunities to observe and adjust and teach in actual classes with a range of bodies. After I taught, she would prompt my reflections on my teaching, and also on the specific bodies that I had contact with during that class. Observation and presence were key elements in her teaching, and she showed me their importance by example. I recall the first time I ever witnessed her kneel down next to someone's body, in a pose, and contemplate it, as though looking for the internal logic of that body in the pose. I was impressed with the strategy and also felt as though I was witnessing something rare—not just in a yoga class but also in regular life: the ability to be present to the truth of another person's body.

What I didn't see, and what I try to eschew in my own classes, is fear. If I don't know how to teach a certain body how to do yoga, I look to that body for cues. I do my informed and intuitive best. If a student becomes a regular in my class, I take the invitation to learn more about the specifics of that body. How does that person's cerebral palsy affect the yoga practice? How does that person's fat distribution affect the yoga practice? How does that person's inflexibility affect the yoga practice? We are not just teaching poses, after all. We're teaching people.

I also learned from the ways in which Sherri managed the entire class climate with regard to student judgments of one another. Establishing the culture of the room is primarily about the teacher, and it also includes the physical setup, how students are allowed or encouraged to interact with each other, and how they refer to or discuss themselves within that setting. For instance, I recall a regular student in our studio who was transitioning her gender, male to female. Over a period of months and years, other students witnessed the changes in her appearance. It's reasonable enough to think that gender should simply not be an issue in yoga, yet the responses from students were a profound reminder that our instruction is always situated in a specific location, in specific bodies and specific cultural interpretations of bodies. As social creatures, we don't escape the burden of making meaning of one another, and this can be profound when also juggling the aims of yoga. We're coming more deeply into our own bodies, after all, putting aside many of our other social identities for a while in favor of participation in the yoga community. That can feel vulnerable to anyone in the room. One day, in class, as we held a seated twist and Sherri came around to provide adjustments to our upright postures, a student who appeared to be male, white, and in his early sixties looked at the transitioning woman with a sneer and in a whisper (intentionally audible to all) said to the teacher, "So, is that a man or a woman?" Sherri answered, calmly but firmly, as she applied her adjustment to the man's spine, "Yes. Now breathe."

This is how class culture is established, little by little. Certain things are encouraged, others are accepted, and some things are not tolerated at all. Based on this culture, the studio attracts its clientele.

In that moment, with the rude (and performative) gender comment, Sherri could've offered more strident comments or asked the speaker to leave the room in order to make a stronger statement in favor of the trans person's comfort. She could've shushed or ignored the speaker. What I saw her convey was that we should focus on our own bodies. It's a message I see and hear in her teaching again and again, and it reframes the idea of whose safety is more important. All of us are unsafe in public, in community, in embodied forms. Indeed, some are more vulnerable to hatred, exclusion, and ridicule—trans women are a prime example. There is no one right way to topple hierarchy, to rid a room of hatred; our bodies and experiences can guide us toward our own ways, and others will join us if they resonate.

Of course, the appropriateness of these interactions depends, in part, on the lineage in which one teaches. In some classes, the student's inner wisdom is thought to be the best guide for modifications. Teaching can be very proscribed. And still, what the teacher chooses to add—or omit—helps to establish the class pedagogy.

Explorations of Beauty and Worthiness

I asked Sherri recently for her reflections on how my body and practice were accepted in the teaching role when I first began offering classes in her studio. Fat yoga and fitness instructors are still not at all the norm at this printing, but we were a downright unusual sight in the 1990s. She replied: "As I think back on that era, I'm not remembering any negative reactions or comments. What I do recall is that some people commented on your flexibility—that they were impressed! And I remember other comments having to do with your poise and your skill in teaching a comprehensive practice session. So—a positive experience is what people reported back to me."

Predictably, part of my acceptance in the teacher role had to do with my physical abilities. The super-capable fat body, especially one that can do unexpectedly laudable things involving strength and focus, is often temporarily exempted from the usual ridicule fat bodies receive. I've sometimes additionally felt students use me as "inspiration porn," which is quite different from simply finding my practice holistically empowering. The term "inspiration porn" is often used to describe feelings of gratitude, relief, or empowerment when viewing disabled people accomplish heroic or even common tasks with courage, grace, and aplomb. I didn't specifically feel that students viewed me that way in Sherri's studio, though I have felt it on occasion since then. At the retreat center where I currently teach, I've had students who—thinking they're saying something complimentary—tell me that if I can love my body, then surely they can too. Or that if I can do a headstand, then there's still hope for them too. There's a certain starry-eyed, "wow, I guess I have nothing to complain about" element in these comments.

Actual appreciation and admiration for me as a mentor is also sometimes present and has a different feel entirely. For instance, Sherri commented on her own process of deciding that I was ready to teach in her studio. She said, "I could tell you had a steady practice yourself and that you had, additionally, the awareness and insight, the sensitivity and knowledge to begin teaching. I definitely loved that you had the courage to step into the teacher role for me—the courage and the confidence to face head-on whatever thoughts the students might have going on inside of them."

These elements are not about the body, yet the body is always in play. It's possible for multiple and even conflicting perceptions to play out at once. Recently, a student who was new to my class scrutinized my posture in a way I found familiar and then gaped with disbelief when she couldn't do what I was doing. This type of response to my body in the teacher role comes up infrequently and fairly predictably nonetheless. She seemed to think that she was failing because I (a fat woman) could do something she couldn't. It's easy to see how this mind-set can arise. Our culture has taught us that bodies line up along a hierarchy of worth, and fat bodies are among the most devalued. If the fat yogi or the old yogi or the disabled yogi can do something considered "advanced," chances are, it's impressive to most.

Sometimes it's simply not possible for clear instructions or a steady practice or even the authority of the role to override the culturally sanctioned dismissal and derision of the fat body. Again, the culture of the yoga studio can either confirm or reconstruct the cultural norms and values we've been given, regarding bodies. As Sherri shared, "The fact that you were a very regular part of the group classes I taught and that many of the students at my studio knew you, I feel, helped a lot in them accepting you into the role of the one leading the class. And for sure they saw me treat you with respect as I did them... So all of those factors helped the transition to be smooth."

She further commented on how students bring their own bodies and ideas about bodies and cultural values into the yoga studio, and on the value in my body's ability to disrupt negative norms. "I loved that you with your big, beautiful, graceful, and limber body just broke all to pieces the *Yoga Journal* image of what a yoga teacher was supposed to look like... One of the biggest comforts for me when you were holding the space in my absence was that I knew you would be competent in handling whatever came up among the students—whatever the particular dynamics would be for a given group, I was sure you'd be able to direct in a good way. That's such a key strength for any teacher to have, you know? The ability to stay calm, to stay engaged, to move the group forward through weird comments or off-colored jokes or who knows what, and to bring the class to a successful completion."

What does it mean for a yoga class to come to a successful completion? I often comment about how much of what we do on the mat is a metaphor for other areas of our lives. Balance, steadiness, strength, flexibility—we take them all with us into our other endeavors. Awareness and practice help make this so.

When it comes to "fat pedagogy," somehow I want to ask students: Are you able to see beauty in me, in my body? And what does that do for your ability to see beauty in yourself? How do we approach one another with the same appreciation (or even reverence) with which we approach nature, the forms of beauty that we can most readily recognize?

When it comes to everyday things like yoga, sex, movement, athleticism, eating, dancing, et cetera, what matters is the *experience* of the body, not the *appearance* of the body. Yes, we have to reject the whole media machine (and sometimes friends and family) to truly grasp this. And it's vital to a good life and a better world. Of course, appearance seems to matter, because there are well-documented rewards and privileges attached to all types of culturally normative appearance. There's no wisdom in staying out of the body's experience, though, no deep pleasure or understanding. It only makes us easier for others to control when we seek privilege and revel in the kind of hierarchies that prop up our sense of self-worth. I realize that people don't like to think of themselves as controllable, but we are. We need community. It's the wisdom of the body, the wisdom of experiencing the body, that can lead us out of all manner of trouble when we fall in. It can lead us to stronger community, wiser culture. Again and again, in our continuing social evolution.

14.

LANGUAGE, QUEER HISTORY, AND MISOGYNY

The word "lesbian" in the title of the caucus was starting to feel a bit archaic to some. Did everyone relate, we wondered, thinking about students and younger academics in particular. Further, would people shy away from this group if their research included women who have sex with women but they themselves were not lesbians?

Fair questions for a "lesbian caucus" to take up at an academic conference. We decided to see who was in the room, so a round of introductions ensued. I spoke my name and scholarly interests and added simply, "I'm queer. I'm a femme dyke."

The next three people in the circle were in their early twenties, perhaps late teens. The first looked at me in surprise and blurted, "Wow, femme dyke! How old-fashioned!" I raised my eyebrows, and a few in the circle looked away awkwardly. The friend next to her tried to clean up that comment but just dug in deeper, saying, "It's just, nobody says that combination of things anymore."

I guffawed, to the relief of the twenty-some people assembled and said to the group, "Correction! I'm a femme dyke and also, apparently, a fucking relic!"

Seeing no real anger in my demeanor, the young woman who spoke said "Sorry!" sheepishly and then went on to introduce herself too. "Queer. Genderqueer. Pronouns: she, her."

That was a far more, ahem, contemporary answer than my own, and the responses around the room definitely would've scattered as you'd imagine on an age graph. Truly, in these fast-paced gender-evolving times, "femme dyke" is a time marker of sorts. I was an adult in the '90s. I wonder, however, if she knew how that identity stood in opposition to the more generic term "lesbian?" What does she know of language and history, and does it even matter? Young people are often placed outside of history, inventing everything, unaware of how their inventions hang like beads on the same strand with those before them. At that gathering, we were all either scholars or students, and that leads to the prevalence of certain identities as well. I recall my ex—maybe a decade ago—responding to someone who asked if she identified as queer. She said, "Nah. That's not my word. That's for the young kids and the intellectuals [she motioned to me]. I'm just a butch dyke."

Whatever small shock and offense I took when that young caucus-attendee treated me like a garish but quaint tea cozy one finds in a thrift store came from feeling dismissed age-wise, not being misunderstood gender-wise. The truth is, I found her friend hot. Not like I was going to hit on her, but most of the time I walk around seeing the world as though I'm young and interesting to others, admiring and imagining others' lives as though I'm the center of my universe. Because I am. It's jarring at times when young queer people see me as a mama rather than as a peer. But I get it. That's accurate. Though nowhere near elderly, I'm definitely an elder. I've been thinking—and then writing and performing—about gender, gender identity, sexuality, preferences, and orientations since I first had a same-sex lover more than thirty-five years ago.

I have skin in the game.

I did not feel shock or offense at that speaker's dismissal of my identity. Truly, I didn't. I'm thrilled by the multiplication of gender nowadays and over the past decade in particular. While I have historically bemoaned the invisibility of femme queerness in public, I always used to say that privately, in queer community, I got respect. I'm not sure that's always true anymore. Sure, I'm respectable based on some people's favorable reading of my work as an individual thinker, but is the "femme dyke" identity as respectable as it once was within communities of people whom outsiders might call gender/sexuality deviant? Do we even recognize each other as part of the same group anymore?

Age is changing my perspective; I don't know. What I do know is that our cultural default of misogyny does not disappear from our unconscious biases, or language usage, without conscious effort.

I remember when gender was fun. We turned it into a toy, a triumph, a question, a tool. We weren't like those poor fuckers who took gender for real, living out the stereotypes without any thought of their origins and consequences. We had compassion for those who struggled to understand, even as we flamboyantly manipulated the misunderstandings and malfeasances of gender in public places. I'm sure gender is still fun for some, but is it compassionate among queer, genderqueer, and homosexual folks? There seems to be more finger-pointing and name-calling, arguing and yelling—actual life and death consequences at times—than in my youth. Or perhaps that's the perspective of age.

How many times in my life have I intervened on behalf of a date (or even a stranger) in a public place who's about to be hassled or harmed going into a public toilet? A lot, that's how many. And those interventions are always based on my read of the harasser's perceptions of my date, and of me, and of themselves, and of how best to cajole an outcome rather than forcing one. I've done the same with trans women friends, cozying up to include, when a harasser seems to want to make us different. That's femme finesse, kin to the Southern Belle insult that leaves you feeling smeared in syrup rather than slapped in the face. That's one form of mediation, and it's a fine point in my quiver.

The foe in those moments was always clear. And perhaps it's not always so these days. I am, after all, a lesbian of a certain age and could hold trans-exclusionary views, upon first glance. My performance of femme has toned down a bit over the years, and I find myself rushing to distance from those who would exclude our trans kin. How tragic and odd that it's come to this. Much like when I travel abroad, I try to distance my Americanness from the U.S. government as soon as possible in conversations with locals. Those who look like me—or maybe it's important to say: those who enjoy my privileges—have done so much to harm others. I still find it unfathomable that trans-exclusionary lesbians are now in cahoots with the likes of fundamentalist groups like

Focus on the Family because somehow they have common aims about whose humanity they'd like to deny.

Perhaps it's the threat and reality of consequences that cause so many queer folks to find gender painful these days. I feel what Sarah Schulman calls "the duty of repair." Being misunderstood is painful. Feeling left out is an insult, difficult to bear, rather than a call to artful construction of something new. A friend commented on my notion of being "left out" by saying, "isn't it more like pushed out? There's actually some violence involved." I'm not sure I agree, though the comment prompts a certain sadness in my body.

How much is fear like fear like fear, across identities falling like dominos into the abyss of fascism? (Really? Lesbian "feminists" feeling kindred with Christian fundamentalists?) Whose fears are justified and whose are nonsense? I think I know, but fear sometimes steers me too. I'm still trying to understand, lest I begin to exclude people with whom I'm somehow kindred.

"I just want to be treated like a normal boy," a young trans man said to me recently. On one hand, I understood. On the other hand, I wondered how normalcy ever became the prize for which some will spend all day throwing the same ball at the county fair. There is a paradox here, no doubt. It's absolutely right to call attention to and make reforms that would shut down the whole bathroom-anxiety story. I work for that too. And at the same time, what does normalcy get us? How can we avoid right-and-wrong constructs altogether and remember the compassion of timing and tolerance for those who just don't see things the same way we do? How do we keep our good humor and love light shining?

Getting It "Right"

I used to perform a rather controversial solo play called *Dykeotomy*. I workshopped it in 2007, and it debuted and then toured in 2009. It was billed as "a funny, erotic game of gender-dodge-ball." I stopped performing it because time had marched on with regard to gendered interactions and language choices and also because I felt a bit too battered at times by the show's responses. That show proceeds from the perspective of a middle-aged femme dyke who's navigating what rampant gender-slippage means to her own dating experiences. It's a comedic social analysis—as are all my plays—written for effect, not personal confession. As with every narrative I present, that character is part me, part collective voice. I write performance scripts ethnographically and autoethnographically. That is, I'm writing about myself in order to understand the culture. In many cases, I'm presenting amalgamations of broader dialogue I've heard on very personal themes. And then, via the audience response, I learn even more about what I've gotten "right" and what stirs discontent.

With regard to "getting it right while stirring discontent," I'd say *Dykeotomy* was one of my three most successful shows ever. Queer and lesbian femmes, along with the butches and trans men who care about them, validated the complexity of the themes and intersections they saw in that show night after night. Because I performed *Dykeotomy* in different countries, one trans man commented, after befriending me on Facebook, "Wow, *Dykeotomy* has turned your Facebook page into the biggest international trans-male support group around!"

At the same time, some expressed anger—not only at the show but also at me. Stunned and always pained by comments that often began with "how dare you," I learned that some audience members thought I was speaking out of turn, that my claims on queer and genderqueer experiences were spurious. I was an outsider. In one city, Butch-Femme-Trans, a group that had agreed to promote the show withdrew their support without even telling me (causing financial as well as personal difficulty) because one of its members thought the show was "problematic."

Since when is that a bad thing? Every single show I write foments discontent! If I've not offered something charming yet highly disturbing, I don't feel I've done my job. Since when do we want to shut down the variety of queer perspectives rather than engage them? (Answering that question could be a whole different essay.)

So what this really comes down to is this: who is entitled to create queer culture and steward queer community? Who gets to be in the driver's seat when it comes to language and definitions and naming and direction? Perhaps I was wrong all along to think that we could learn to take turns, read the map together. We each know the same landscape differently, so it seems we've all something to learn from our embodied experience. After all, if a group is called Butch-Femme-Trans, I am a bona fide third of that label, though sadly sometimes seen as a silent partner. There are already culturally prescribed hierarchies that we can't always see we're following. Unless we work against it, femmes will always be silenced in favor of the "real" queer voices.

As Sarah Schulman says, in her book, *Conflict Is Not Abuse*, "Confusing being mortal with being threatened can occur in any realm. The fact that something could go wrong does not mean that we are in danger. It means we are alive." On social media especially, it's much easier to call out views and assign "permanently damaged" status to people. It makes them easier to "cancel," but then, surprise! Problematic views can arise elsewhere. Just as calling someone a racist can actually let the person off the hook for specific racist things they said or did, canceling someone excludes without creating remedy.

My practice is not to dismiss those with whom I disagree (though sometimes it's good to take a little space). I realize that loving the opposition isn't everyone's calling, nor should it be, but it is my calling. I keep coming back, particularly to those with whom I've had challenging discussions. That includes those with whom my views diverge and those with whom I share interests, labels, and aims despite disagreement. Often, when it seems we should be showing solidarity and fortifying our focus on bigger foes, we are wounding one another with verbal skewers and exclusions.

A colleague confronted me a few years back about a sentence I'd used in a story I wrote and whether or not I'd considered the damage it might do to a transgender reader who could feel unattractive or even excluded from queer community as a result. The line was "I want a man who remembers having been a little girl."

Could I have used more inclusive language to make my point? I considered this. I really did. At first, it took me a little while to understand the critique. We conversed awkwardly in my slowness. This colleague, also a writer and performer, prompted me to consider the power of the stage. Indeed, I agree that platform has power—and that's just why we need to use it to present complex truths, not binary thinking. I agreed with my colleague that sometimes people see a person on the stage as an authority. Could I be more inclusive?

As my mind played back over our exchange, I wondered at my irritation. I felt I'd been chastised for not saying the "right" thing, as if somehow I'd missed the queer stakeholders meeting and hadn't read my minutes. Dude, I wish I'd said, I know what the "right" thing is and it is rarely interesting. Sometimes it's useful to artfully say the right thing. I find this writer deft at that task. And art can do more. It can represent what isn't popular in ways that prompt uncomfortable discovery, for starters. It can put out into public the things that may often be said only in private or only by a villain or only by the eye-rollingly dismissible ingénue. But what if someone respectable, loveable even, is standing up for complexity? That's what I'm going for. Then suddenly the irony of the audience member's role is being revealed. The paradox is that we are each acting and watching, sometimes suddenly being revealed, then scrutinized, then invisible.

Few things are as frightening to me as the entrenchment of dichotomous thinking. The United States has done this (unwittingly?) with the two-party political system and majority rule voting. If one side is right, the mind too easily says, then the other must be wrong. No line item veto, despite how one might try to explain and add nuance. Or is anyone really doing that in an age of politicians being coached for how to reach specific constituents with language patterns, pauses, and glances? Many of us decide with whom we wish to be allied before even opening our minds to an opinion. Those people with trans-exclusionary views must surely feel dismissed by the LGBT community. They have been, because their exclusionary views are rabidly incorrect. Still, how must that feel and what strange venom and allies does that isolation produce?

One of language's functions is to delineate. To state that the blue of the sunny sky is different than the blue of dusk nearing night. Using the nuances of language, we can say that things are alike and different and prompt emotions that give us both pause and then power to ask, "what was meant by that?" This is what I hope when I use language that people generally keep in private. If we are unpacking sex and gender, it seems right to state a view that says what one might want from another. There's meaning in how attractions emerge based on others' life experiences. We are not equally attracted to everyone, after all, nor are we attracted to simple human musk. There is meaning to be discovered in the nuances of cherished identities, appearances, and attractions. Juxtapositions point to the ephemeral and shifting aspects of being human.

I use language to include and to delineate and also to prompt questions. In particular, I want to eschew the idea that there is one right way to talk about things like gender and sex, gender identity, and sexual attraction. The first person voice makes it sound briefly like one person is speaking alone, but it's never so. I want to explore "what is" in its various meanings and nuances, rather than simply stating "what should be" according to best practice or good manners, or contemporary rhetoric or human dignity or anything else. Sometimes I use language to summarize and recommend. Other times, language can complicate, separate, and even obfuscate in service of further discovering the nuances of human thought and behavior.

Alone and in Relation

We exist as both subjects and objects of our own identities. I have been a femme dyke since the first time that woman kissed me, more than thirty-five years ago. I have been other things too with my lovers. I occasionally belong to categories containing such types as "lesbians" and "girls" and "mamas" and "active bottoms" (also the term for exercise pants at a store where I shop). Language is referential in multiple ways. Sure, a person can have a gender identity independent of attraction to others. And humans do not live in isolation; we're social. To my mind, there's no wrong way to play and learn and love together. There is only information about who we are, where we've come from, and what we might create.

We come from brutal places. The desire for "normalcy" is often a desire for privilege. "I just want to be treated like a normal boy" does not usually mean, "I want to learn how to not cry. I want to learn to talk over women and render them meaningless in my life. I want to feel nothing when tragedy comes through me like a hurricane." But wanting normalcy can sometimes contain the assumption of having missed out on an easier life that was somehow your right, now denied. Whatever axis of identity removed the privilege can be reviled. Rather than hating the loss of dignity wherever it occurs, hating the feeling of "abnormal" is the neoliberal answer. Just let me be me, as though me is singular and unrelated.

Cooper Lee Bombardier's book, *Pass with Care*, explores the interrelationship of trans and queer and dyke identities and how placing oneself too firmly in any identity can cause lack of relationship in the others. Sometimes, it can cause lack of fulfillment in oneself. We need more creative explorations of ambiguity—in marginalized subcultures and in the broader culture too. The navigation of these schisms is not simply a quest related to gender. The desire to feel right in one's body plagues people in different ways, and it has been set up to plague us through social hierarchy, cultural expectations, the pursuit of privilege, and an unnecessary, widespread poverty in a time of economic abundance. The current neoliberal pursuit of personal solutions for cultural problems is manifold. Drug-induced and surgical body modifications can also be discussed as a category independent of gender. The urge to modify—whether it's breast enhancement or removal—is not wrong. How could it be, given the fact of personal sovereignty. It is also culturally situated. We need more stories, more perspectives drawing patterns, and wobbly lines around categories of like and difference. The thing I love best about our current cultural multiplication of gender is that it reminds us: we possess greater human diversity and potential than we can even name.

I recently took up an intellectual flirtation with someone, in which it quickly became hard to discern whether we were actually flirting or just thinking and talking about sex and gender together. I realize I often throw it all in the same mortar and then pestle away, so who knows if we were doing sex or thinking. (Note: she later said it was sex.) She reported being asked about her gender identity and was pondering her snap response: "she/her and they/them." Then she realized these words did not answer the question. She identified with the word "boi." So I asked. "What do you like about it?"

"It's a masculine signifier, " she said, "but with the edges rounded out—because I'm definitely not butch!"

After a pause indicating that was all, I gingerly asked what I always wonder regarding the popularity of this term "boi." "So, that speaks to the gender aspect of the word 'boy,' but what about the part of that word that also means 'child.' How do you relate to that? I mean, other than in wanting to maintain a sense of playfulness." I spoke the obvious connotation with "boyishness" before she could default to it.

"Well playfulness is what I thought of when you first said it—but I don't think I've ever thought about that 'child' meaning before!" She seemed surprised. "But, yes, clearly, even if I'm spelling it b-o-i, there's a pre-existing meaning attached to that word…"

"And it's all being pulled into the new meaning you create—otherwise, you'd use a different word." I finished her thought, because I'm eager that way. "I mean look, there's a reason why 'femme' is related to and separate from 'femininity' and we constantly talk about the two terms in relationship. I so rarely hear people who identify as 'boi' unpack what the child aspect of that means to them."

By the end of the conversation, she said she didn't like that term for self-reference anymore. I said, "Aw, I didn't mean to put you off your gender identity!" To which she/they replied, "Well, that's just what you've done. Intention means nothing!" And we had a good laugh, as I always hope we will.

Meaning and Reference

We have to agree that language means something. It's representative, after all, never the actual thing it's standing in for. When discussing identity, we are the things being described, and we are constantly in motion. Even when sitting in stillness, the body is always moving—eyes fluttering, heart beating, cells vibrating. We are growing and decaying, and when we rub one word out on a page, it leaves a trace. The word palimpsest has its origins in Greece, where writing surfaces were used again and again. It means rubbed smooth again.

We don't really *have to* agree that language is referential. We already have. Femme is not feminine but references it. Butch is not masculine, but it references a type of masculinity that is hard-won and maybe defiant. A type of masculinity that can be inscribed by a word but not totally defined by it. The word "boy" means male child, but a boi is something like a man, the way a grown woman with short hair and a masculine stance, in a suit or jeans and T-shirt often looks like an adolescent boy, a young man, only softer. How did "boi" erase "soft butch"? And why are we not discussing the rest of the meaning the word "boy" carries?

I want to always remember that, even though our queer histories have not been writ large in culture, we are part of a broader tapestry of self-making, sex-making, love-and-lusting family-making. It stretches through all of time. I don't see how it could be otherwise. If I'm not careful, I too behave as the young college students at the beginning of this essay, as though I know what's quaint, what's radical, and whom to admire, based on appearance alone. Of course we are most familiar with our own predilections, but it's time to habituate the effort to see further than our own classrooms, bedrooms, dungeons, time periods, nations, and even species.

I have been fierce femme, sexy mama, big mama. Only rarely is Mama, writ large, considered sexy. I'm a planner-caretaker in a fertility fetish body. I started out as an ample Snake Goddess and am aging into the Venus of Willendorf. I have what some have called "physical credibility" to go along with my identity leanings.

A past lover whom I called Daddy scoffed once at another self-made Daddy, slight of build, short. "No physical credibility," she said. Of course, the speaker was nearly six self-aggrandizing feet tall, body-builder muscles. I called her Daddy, and I mothered her as well, but she never said the word "mother." The comfort provided by women is meant to be invisible, unspoken. Further, "mother" has been de-eroticized, even though mother is the earth, the round hills, the sweet breeze on sweaty skin, the salt and musk of bodies made by coupling.

Everything we say is referential to misogyny as well, even though we think we are talking ourselves out of that trap.

Opting out of pain and complexity is the particular brand of normalcy we seek. The perfect privilege of male innocence equates to normal in our culture. And we never have to talk about it. Maleness is never meant to be accountable to the damage it does to non-men. That's the social pact: we are never expected to talk about what is "normal." Normalcy comes with its own entitlement to privacy.

When I think of someone who's "soft butch," I still picture an adult who might manage a mortgage, clean the rain gutters, then make dinner. Bois might be wrestling in the park or out on the town hitting a few strip bars, like men whose first responsibility is always to their own pleasure.

I made an offhand joke once, long ago, from the stage at a primarily queer venue. A small group in the audience—pals by the look of it—had identified themselves as bois and I vamped. "B-o-i, I suppose?" There was nodding and laughter. The term was becoming common but was still new. I quipped coquettishly to the audience, "Well, they're cute, but what's happening with all these bois who never grow up? Give me a full grown butch any day. Mama's tired and needs a little help fixing the world." The audience howled, punctuated by some particularly deep hoots which I imagined to be validation from my butch fans.

Neither body modification nor identity modification are new—neither is renaming, for that matter. I wish to never speak of trans-exclusionary women again, yet there's something about living that draws us into conflict, makes us feel the small hairs rise whether or not the fight arrives. Kai Cheng Thom (in "Why Are Queer People So Mean to One Another") discusses how queer communities act from trauma pathways since we share a marginalization that makes everyone look like a threat. Generative conflict is the key, though; we cannot sustain ourselves on call-outs. I don't let other bigots hijack my choice of topic and style of discussion; why is it so easy to allow when discussing trans-exclusion (which I do not consent to call feminist)?

My identity as a femme dyke—or lesbian, as I've often been called and feel fine about—can be claimed independent of external definition, but we are all so easily suspicious of each other, it seems. "We," in this case, means marginalized non-male people, because few people seem to be calling out, or trying to disassociate from, gay men who think poorly of trans women, cis-women, straight women, and queer women of all stripes. There are still gay men who don't associate with women, openly joke about how disgusting we are, and do not invite us to their homes. These men remain "part of our community." They sit on community boards representing LGBT issues, and sometimes (because money can enable segregationist views) they're respected donors to gay causes. Misogyny is largely unnoticed in so many corners of culture, including those that claim to be liberatory, after all. I'm not trying to argue that trans-exclusionary women are a trivial problem here, rather they are one face of misogyny and bigotry. We have not yet handled gay misogyny or the homophobia and body-policing ("no fats, no femmes") that keeps gender deviants unsafe. We have not yet handled body sovereignty—my broader aim. "Love wins" was always going to be an easy end, but what of sex and gluttony, of the types that are unsavory to most? We must claim dignity for all, but are we even reaching for it? Body sovereignty is the brass ring on the merry-go-round of acceptance and respectability.

The most disturbing thing about trans-exclusionary views is how rigidly dogmatic and somehow mainstream they've become. Indeed, I view these perspectives as part of the current zeitgeist in which conspiracy theories and fear are at a fever pitch. If someone had told me, thirty years ago, that people calling themselves lesbians (and radical lesbians at that—a term originally flagging critique of capitalism) would ally with right-wing politicians against trans interests, I'd have wondered how that came to be. Yet, here we are. There are women in my social media feed who argue with me on these points and who are genuinely oblivious to how their warped logic fits nicely with certain fascist and right-wing media tirades.

I stand solidly in favor of the explosion of gender and love for my trans kin. And also, I want to assert the multiplicity of themes related to sex, gender, sexuality, and naming. I want to discuss where neoliberal and fascist leanings lurk—even in trans-ideologies. I want a broader discussion, as Paul Preciado put forth in *Testo Junkie*, of the medicalization of gender, especially as it plays into the past definitions of women's bodies as deficient and requiring medical/male establishment intervention. There is so much to discuss! If all we ever do is leap to align ourselves with the "right" answers, we're re-entrenching good and evil in imitation of the broader culture in ways that are both dangerous and dull. I don't want to be so focused on having the prettiest party dress at the picnic that I don't notice the ants carried off the meal hours ago.

Paradoxically, I think broader discussions might help us find common ground on narrow issues. I understand the urge to unfriend those whom I find unhinged and abusive, and I don't do it on social media because I want to understand the times in which I live, learn my own blind spots and continue to respect others. Even those with whom I don't agree. I also want to stay close enough to those who might lash out that I can move defensively to protect my loved ones when needed. What a strange world in which we live when different types of lesbians find more fault with one another than with the broader systems that oppress us.

But wait, of course we've been here before. I've been called the "straight lady" at lesbian events aplenty and shunned as a "tourist." Even recently, I attended a Pride event in a small town and felt that I still don't fit in. While I might've flirted with some of those women in their fifties and sixties, some were still looking at me like a tourist, an ally, a straight lady. It seems like we should've moved past that—feminine women represent lesbians all over popular media, but still, without a *real* dyke on my arm, I'm invisible. The younger folks at that Pride event seemed to be a gender-ambiguous cuddle-puddle of plush unicorns and glitter. Goddess bless their cute cotton socks.

There just aren't many folks like me. I'm still a particular brand of femme—reclaimed femininity, gritty and sometimes sophisticated, ready to intervene against bigotry when I see it yet somehow easily erased. Not queer enough. Not nonbinary enough. Not even interesting enough for advertisers to sell my image back to me in beer ads. Those two women in wedding gowns in the insurance commercials were never meant to read as femme, by the way. Maybe you can't tell, but I can. They're mainstream white ladies who just want their ding-dang rights to marry another gal. I want to fuck for fun, fight for fairness, and finagle a better world until my last breath. See the difference?

There's something in all of this that makes me want to ask: Can we stop taking ourselves so seriously and thinking that we have all the right answers? When someone disagrees, or points out another view, or says something that seems "offensive," can we stop being so miserable and uptight over it—maybe even stay open to learning something? At the very least, can we re-remember that queer community contains every experience of the world? We do not touch or handle queerness without pushing against class and race, size/ability/age stigma, and so on. We have to keep expanding our understanding of other's experiences.

There's something in all of this that makes me want to ask: Can we start taking ourselves more seriously? Femme can't be about glitter and tiaras and prom queen adoration all the time. The girly-girls and bois have real work to do creating the culture that honors not just them but every version of them and others yet to come. There's work involved in ending misogyny and racism and oppressions of every kind. Playful, creative, intense, joy-loving work to be done.

Naming can be fun. We create conflict, safety, bravery, and other responses in turn and maybe sometimes all at once. We contain multitudes. We are constantly reinventing—both as normal and in opposition to normal, in order to bump out the boundaries on respectable human experiences. We claim the unloved and exalted parts of ourselves through naming and respecting others. And maybe that's been the point, all along.

15.

THREE, TWO, ONE

Jim and I were on the phone, discussing his recent love gone wrong, and, boy, did he feel like shit. He wondered if it'd be possible to have a do-over for that threesome. Get it right.

And I wondered if it was possible for the sex to go wrong. Or is it always the relationships that go wrong and cause the sex to falter? I mean, barring force, coercion, infection or ... can sex go wrong? Or is it the relationships?

The do-over would be reparative, Jim explained. They'd invite that guy back again for another threesome. Jim had it worked out in his head. They could fuck him like this, or like that. Make eye contact with each other at just the right moment. Get everyone in the groove.

I listened. Unconvinced. Even Jim was not convinced as he made the argument.

"But sometimes there's such ecstasy in a threesome," said Jim. "I mean, when it's great, it's great. And when it's not?"

My mind answered the question: There's emotional turmoil and feelings of inadequacy or disrespect or abandonment, and you think about it for days, weeks, months. Had it been a year since their first go of it? He added, "The problem wasn't the threesome."

I nodded, on the phone, when he said it.

Really? Jim met Mr. Threesome for drinks just to get his take on the situation, even after Jim and his partner had parted ways. From the invited guest's point of view, everything was great. Mr. Threesome is involved in his own drama with his husband divorcing him to move to Brazil with a younger man, though. Yeah, definitely, everything was great.

It's sort of a miracle when two people make enough of the same story of their interactions, their looks, their words, and alliances in order to have a good experience, settle down, and enjoy some time. Definitely a miracle to make it last.

During the lengthy catch-up with Jim, I have also begun thinking about the most recent person I dated. Just a week, then friendship. "Flirtatious friendship," she said.

"What are you getting out of that?" I grumped.

Something had gone wrong. Or maybe it went right. How could I know which?

About a year ago, I overheard a conversation that has stayed with me. I was in a gallery where a woman's art was being shown, and someone smiled and marveled at her domestic feat—she and her husband: forty years together this year! Her husband said, "Yeah, no trick, really. If you're lucky to meet someone when you're both young enough, you grow up together. All of your likes and dislikes develop together. How you handle things. You know what the other person means. That makes it easy. We get along. " They both smiled and nodded, like a postcard image from the land of happy relationships.

Maybe it's lucky that I still have some growing up to do.

See how I did that? Went straight to optimism rather than saying, *god, you're screwed really, if you try to partner up as an adult, an older adult, an adult with your own ways of coping and finding beauty in the world, thank you very much. Don't harsh my mellow, babe.* I already know how things work. One could see it like that instead. I'm always so fucking optimistic.

"Doesn't there have to be some kind of effortless frisson in a good threesome?" I said to Jim. "Or some kind of arduous planning? I mean, as soon as you're trying to *make* it go well, it's already not going well. So, the do-over would never work. The two of you with the plan would be maneuvering the third in order to get it right. And then that third guy—that guy who's not part of your relationship, that guy who's really great and really hot and carrying around his own drama—that guy's just a prop.

"I don't relate to sex like that," I said to Jim.

• • •

But, of course, sometimes I do. I'm always telling some kind of story in my head—I think everyone does that. I am also feeling the body. And perceiving the other person. It's not like we respond to one another based on scent alone We have interconnected stories. Sometimes our stories rub each other the wrong way, though there can be attraction in that too. And what about emotions? Always a river of emotion just beneath the skin. A grip that leaves bruising can mean pleasure, and the most tender touch, pain. An embrace soothes one day, stifles the next. The lexicon is unstable. It's amazing we ever understand each other at all. Perhaps the range of human stories is smaller than I'm willing to admit.

"You showed me tenderness," my date said.

And I learned that was a bad thing. Only not bad, because, wow, who would call that bad? I didn't even know what I'd done that could be interpreted as tender. I'm just being ... human, I thought. But, yeah, that can look a lot of ways. Tenderness caused distance, which wasn't what I was hoping for. It wasn't what she wanted either, at least not at first. She was so interested in me at first—and remains so, though in an oddly constructed sort of way. I pouted and pondered. Then I laughed at myself. Always back to compassion and amusement, still a little weird and nervous; hopeful me.

Even with two. Even with one. We are telling ourselves our stories. My body and mind don't always know each other. Emotions spring from both, make a wet mess or a happy puddle. How can it feel so good to sleep in the wet, metal, acid, musty funk of sex, body truly relaxed? Body rent, spent, heavy with sleep, still whole. Is "good sex" even about knowing someone or just imagining what we mean to each other, what we ourselves have become, with the other?

I've felt alone in a loved one's embrace too.

"I have issues with trust," my date said. I was listening and trying to understand, but I didn't understand. Why would a person let that shit win? Yeah, so what? That's my story. Maybe I was not listening well enough. Try again. Stop. Don't try too hard to understand. I could just listen. Was I listening or telling my own story? I couldn't tell.

• • •

Here's a story about a threesome that went wrong. Jim keeps talking about the sex gone wrong like it's the important part. And my mind is traveling.

This was a long time ago so I have nothing but perspective, which is all I ever really had even when it was happening: mine. I am just one person after all.

Two of us were long-term lovers, thinking that we already knew each other. We didn't know ourselves in *that* situation. I'm not sure I know us now, so I'm grateful that the past is pliable and lets me remold it according to my current understanding. This is the story that came to mind when Jim was saying, "What if we could just have a do-over? Maybe then it would all turn out okay." Maybe then Jim wouldn't be meeting his former partner in the park, for a walk, rather than wasting another meal he couldn't eat after those kinds of awful conversations they have now. We are so easily damaged by intimacy—so often remade by it as well.

My lover was an angry, jealous sort. And, wow, that can take up a lot of time and supplant ease and many of the good feelings people have for one another. She perceived an interloper, interested in my affections. I rolled my eyes. Tedious. "So what if she's hot for me?" I said about the interloper. "I can't do anything about that." I said. "I'm totally not into her or I'd have already done something about it!" I made a bold statement. I wouldn't let her think she was bullying me. I'd have had sex with the interloper if I wanted to. I didn't want to.

(My eleven-year-old son laid it down for me once, after an evening we spent with this same interloper: "You're stupid if you don't know she likes you."

I replied, "I know she likes me, but what can I do about that?"

He answered with the buggy eyes of a kid who had to tolerate adult stupidity. "You could stop encouraging her!")

So, my lover and I were on a road trip, and I was starting to get pouty about the whole trip blown to hell because of her jealousy and nonsense, and soon she'd go stoic and not even speak to me. But then something different happened. She said, "Okay, what if I do something else with this feeling? What if I embrace it? What if I see it for what it is: someone thinks you're hot. Why wouldn't she? I think you're hot!" I brightened a bit. Could this be? She continued. "Yeah, she and I are alike enough that I could totally even see what she's into about you. Yeah, I like her! I mean, I do actually like her. It's not like I'm mad at her about anything. I get it. You *are* hot."

Mobility was one of the things I loved about her, the ability to come up out of something tricky and think about it, move to see it another way. It had just never happened before on *this* theme. I was nodding, not minding at all being thought of favorably now by both of these women—the interloper and my lover, with whom I was not going to have a bad weekend after all. Then she said, "Yeah, I'm totally getting into the idea of watching her fuck you."

"Hang on. Are you serious?" I was stunned that she'd gone straight from angry and jealous to *this*. She'd gone straight to watching us fuck from giving me side-eye and saying, "Never a minute's peace with you. Every butch dyke within four hours of here comes sniffing around your porch wondering if you *neeeeed* anything." That old saw exhausted me, of course, and I whined about how they never meant anything by it, but I was not sure her new turn would be an improvement.

It's not that I'm against threesomes. I'm just not a fan. If the moment seemed right, my optimism would likely kick in again, though I'd doubt my competence. In theory, great. It seems like communication is all it takes, but meh. I'd sort of relegated threesomes to youthful experimentation. I'd experimented. I prefer connection and depth with one person, with myself, and, well, whether or not I always get those things has nothing to do with the thrill of a third person.

"But what if something amazing can be enhanced?" Jim said.

"What if it can?" I countered. "At what risk to some greater, longer-lasting peace?"

But, hey, it was fun to see her so animated about something that normally installed a rain cloud over her head. Then it was fun to speculate, with my lover, about the desires and propensities of this third person, to review the small things the lovely interloper said that were evidence of what she would think or want or like or do. My lover and I had a good time on that trip, and good sex, and ease. That's what I want really. Ease. Just let there be ease, kindness, affection. Of course I want good sex. Maybe I want more than I realize.

• • •

Just before our fourth date in one week, the woman with trust issues asked me whether I enjoy affection, somewhat public affection. We both noted the small thrill of our legs leaning together on a previous date, in the theater, and I was thinking about how a small thrill can take up residence and exude a larger loveliness than expected. And about how much I loved the clarity of a direct question like, "Do you enjoy public affection?" And we would be in that theater again that very evening. I am not often one to make bold gestures, but I think, good. I have made space for her simple gestures, bold gestures. I was receptive and looking forward to affection. Quite so. I was possessed of a small thrill, just in the talking. The talking, indeed, was what had happened between us, nothing else. Yet the loveliness was large. But that night something was off. She didn't touch me all evening, even after asking to earlier in the day. Not even her leg leaning into mine.

• • •

By the second day of our road trip, after the swimming and strolling, during the long and scenic drive toward home, my lover and I were planning to ask the interloper (who had then become the "third party," or even the "sweet friend") if she wanted to … you know. How will we ask her, and what mood will be made of this? The planning was a small thrill, growing larger, and we were fairly sure she'd say yes. She'd been doing some work on the house, and that's why my lover became fixated on her in the first place. The two of them worked all morning on the house, and I worked inside and then made lunch, and the three of us ate, and then they got back to work. Every evening when we were alone, my lover fixated on how the interloper looked at me and flirted. And I said no, that kind of flirting didn't mean anything. It was just appreciation, recognition. And my lover curled her lip in disgust.

We were planning the threesome, so sure we knew what was coming, but how on earth could we have known each other, our own minds—let alone her? We were just happy for the relief of jealousy and anger. Well, I was, and perhaps that relief made me extra hopeful, because usually I'm a think-and-talk-things-through kind of gal. And I certainly wouldn't have wanted the interloper, our sweet friend, to be uncomfortable in any way.

I phoned while we were on the road and left a coquettish message saying how we'd been keeping company so much lately, what with the home improvements and all, and that my lover and I had been thinking about her and could we talk soon?

• • •

It's not the who's-doing-what in bed, it seems to me as Jim talks. It's who's looking at whom and how. The flow of the eye contact; the flow of connection. Who feels important and why. It's the wanting and fulfillment of desire for something that's not just physical. I'll accept that some people are better at these encounters than others, and it seems that, for Jim, it's gone well numerous, numerous times. He's a directive sort, after all, and I'm sure he steers well around tight corners, maneuvers out of a cul de sac with ease. Maybe it'd be easier with three strangers, I muse, during our conversation. "No," he says, "it's particularly sweet when two of the people really care for each other." I realize that I've never been "the third" in a threesome. I've always been one of the two partnered people. At some point, I've always thought, *Why are we doing this?* even if the whole thing was … nice.

• • •

The interloper did indeed agree, said she felt like suddenly it was Christmas. I felt my first heart-clench of overwrought expectation.

We had a simple candlelit dinner, and my lover was suave, sexy, and a bit removed. She had already turned voyeuristic. We had discussed nothing of our fantasies with our invited guest. Truth is, I'm not even sure I had my own specific fantasies. Which was strange for us. Usually I was the one steering the romance, though she was driving the sex. I smiled, winked, and beckoned with one painted fingernail; I tapped my shiny lower lip, raised an eyebrow, and she leaned in for a kiss.

This was so different—her imagining and discussing the unfolding event, during our road trip. I was excited hearing all of the setup she envisioned, all of the anticipation she'd mustered. She had really talked it through, and that was the thrill for me. I recalled how, when we were first together, it took her a while to get good at phone sex. I give good talk; she was more action than language.

I'd already had what I wanted. The ease. The talk. The twosome.

Did I mention I wasn't into this woman? I wasn't lying. That was the truth. And as soon as she was kissing me, I panicked. *What the fuck kind of stupid idea was this?* And then she was kissing my lover, and I swear to god my lover was having the same thought because, you know, who invited *that* kiss? Not me. Not her. I've been with women who turn into giant homophobes about the thought of a butch-on-butch kiss. That wasn't it exactly, but what was it? And what was happening to my lover and her assertiveness? As we moved to the bed, as if on a conveyor belt, I was already thinking how to maneuver into the driver's seat. We were careening out of control. I didn't know how weird things had gotten for my lover until she looked at me, stricken, with the interloper kissing down her back, and mouthed, "Help."

Oh, this is good, I thought. And then I started noticing the interloper's energy and how she would turn to me, ravenous, then back to my lover, perfunctory, and I said, "Hey, let me just put words on the dynamic here. I'm not sure there's a charge happening between the two of you in the same way that both of you have a charge for me." And it was like I'd just given two magnets permission to fly apart—but when they both instantly attached onto me with a powerful zeal, I thought, lord help me, what have I done? And who were these sniveling cowards I was in bed with anyway? Neither one of them had any voice of her own.

"I just didn't want you to feel left out," said the interloper to my lover, and they practically shook hands, all forgiven.

It's also true that I felt a sweet protective feeling toward my lover. And that's not totally hot. Then there they were, like a hundred hands and mouths and, okay, she didn't know me, but Jesus, do *not* bite my nipples. Too much was happening at once.

And maybe it's this: Nothing they were doing was about me. It was about them, only not really that either. It was about some idea of each other and some idea of me and some idea I had about ease. And they'd have just carried on, only I'm not keen to be the vessel for something in which I'm not really participating, and so I sat up and said, "I'm very sorry, but this isn't working for me." And I stood up and started putting on a bit of clothing, just enough to be clear, polite. I was apologizing, and my lover sat back to watch me do my thing. She knew me and respected my voice, my sexual intuition, and my sense of things. She often took my lead because she trusted it.

We went back to the table, and I served dessert, and what could we say? Our interloper was apologizing and re-strategizing and trying to get us all back to bed. And I was done. My lover had gone back to her stoic observer role, waiting for me to find the kind and comfortable way out of all this. She was definitely still in her sexuality, but like a vacuum-packed container of her sexual self—no scent of anything, nothing in the package to be affected by the outside air. I knew we'd be doin' it when the interloper left, and the trouble was, the interloper knew it too. She was hurt and felt excluded because she had been. And not just by me.

I'm not sure what happened between the two of them, but they remained friends in the coming months, became closer even, as they sat on the porch and drank beer, my lover affectionate toward me, the interloper a bit chilly to me when she'd say hello or goodbye. It took years before the interloper and I were on truly good terms.

• • •

I've learned this lesson before, in childhood, and how many times since? The person who finds the voice stands to lose the relationships. I'm always trying to grow up enough to find the kindness in the voice. I still stand to lose, even as I soften so my voice doesn't sound like, "Well, fuck you, at least I'm still standing." We are all damaged in interactions where meaning and expectations are unclear, but the one who speaks up becomes the beacon, impossible to ignore, demanding, irritating.

My date said those trust issues weren't about me, and that was some small relief, but she didn't want to keep dating me either. Those issues influenced how close I could be to her. I'm still drawn to her, yet I cannot come near. What use is the attraction? There's some meaning in that word, isn't there? Attraction. Something magnetic, like metal, wood, blood, the scent of sex or purpose. Does purpose have a scent? Does sex have a scent before it happens? Everything contains its opposite too: repulsion. I read once that organically occurring perfumes, like those containing wood or flowers, will always be more compelling to humans than synthetic scents. Synthetic scents are all good-smell. The natural ones also contain feces and decay.

"I'm definitely attracted you. This is all new territory for me," my date said. "I enjoy/adore you, and for whatever reason…" She didn't remain compelled. Or maybe it was that she felt more compelled to withdraw. Not my business to know.

Something was in decay; stillborn. And I was suspiciously eyeing her. Her inability to remain true to a simple attraction made her seem untrustworthy and somehow more interesting. Is that even true? Maybe it's more trustworthy to actually see a person's errant whims and fears, rather than them being hidden. Such strange start-stop inconsistencies and fear-pleasure combinations. I was noting the inconsistencies—in her and in me too. Single. Separate. Still interested. Irritated.

Accepting. Still engaged and observing. What do I care if some stranger doesn't want to date me anymore? The body wants complexity, not just the good. I am attracted to sweet-clear-something-not-quite-right-complexity, already waking up in the warm puddle of it, though alone.

• • •

My life is good. I am alone. In the hammock, I'm listening with interest to Jim's story about his recent loss of love. "We didn't communicate enough," he said.

I said, "It sounds like you communicated all the time; you just didn't want the same things."

He disagreed, and we carried on discussing the terrain of speaking and listening and sometimes deciding to do what doesn't feel right or what feels right in the moment but you know it won't be later.

Jim said, "He knew it would hurt me to leave with the guy from the threesome, and he did it anyway. He even acknowledged it later. He knew he could've simply stopped and connected with me and then called that guy afterward if he was going to do that. That would've been unpleasant, but not the same as leaving with him, barely a goodbye to me."

I sighed at the pain of this. "It wasn't the lack of communication." I said. "It was the follow-through."

Now my date and I only communicate via email. All this speaking and listening and writing and reading, and my erotic body doesn't understand why it's been left out of the conversation. The body is how I know things, and if there's one thing I've learned from this odd bit of dating, my mind shouldn't be in charge. It's too unstable and is far too fond of its own notions. If I'd been Jim, I would've wanted a kiss, touch, and fondness too, before my lover left the house. That scenario makes me want to cry. More zeal for a stranger than kindness for an intimate. More desire to stay separate from someone significant than to risk being close. Even knowing what made sense, Jim's lover couldn't do it. Even with so much spark and talk and enthusiasm, my date decided that even kissing me once, just to find out what attraction was there, would be too much.

Whether it's three, two, or just one person, we learn the shifting terrain of love and sex slowly with a combination of fear and pleasure. Never the same river twice. New bodies and stories bring new meaning.

But the mind *can* maintain the same river, step into it the same way, again and again. The mind can make pleasure or fear, depending on what it expects, creates, endures.

I told a friend about the dates gone wrong and she said, "Don't push the river."

"I'm impatient." I replied. "I want to know what's possible; what's not."

I also know this: Love listens and is patient. Fear wants speedy resolution and will get all up in someone's business to find relief. I have trust issues. But why would a person let that shit win?

I know what I want, and there's risk in it but not too much. I will almost always choose the risk of two, probably not three or more. I am fairly content with one. Jim and I are talking about communication, and that means memory and longing and whether what we want can match up with our abilities to achieve it. When I'm confused, the body tells me when to hang on, when to let go, when to stand up and put my clothes on. That's my story. I trust that wanting means I'm alive. It's good to be alive. I rely on the beauty of being able to stand up again after feeling broken. So far, that's what's always happened.

There's wisdom in optimism. That's my story.

16.

TATTOOS AS THRESHOLDS

Go ahead. Ask. "What's that *mean?*"

My ex-wife taught herself how to tattoo using her own legs for practice. And then her arm, the left one, because she could reach it with the tattoo gun in her right hand. She self-adorned with letters, numbers, old school images, like Sailor Jerry's stuff, and then images with more shading, color, and nuance. She was already a visual artist, with art degrees and everything. This was just another medium, and her skin was a handy canvas. Her legs in particular became a strange jumble of images. I don't think it even occurred to her that this was odd until she went to Las Vegas and was walking around in shorts for a week among a bunch of strangers. She'd mostly been covered up in England, where she had been living and needle-doodling for the previous few years.

Hers was not a usual relationship to tattoos. Sure, some people just emblazon themselves with images they like, images with little meaning to them, but most, it seems, want to have some connection to the image. Tattoos are an ongoing graphic diary of their lives. Or they represent a series of commemorations. The stories people tell about their tattoos and what meaning they make of them have become commonplace forms of communication among people under age forty. The tattooed are a growing in-group, no longer a deviant fringe. People trade tattoo stories in supermarkets and on buses, waiting for their kids at school and changing clothes at the gym. It used to be impolite to ask about someone's tattoo, like you should back off and not ask "that kind of person" something so obviously personal. Now people use compliments about "the artwork" to start conversations or even to initiate touching.

It's an intimacy, a flirtation at times. And it sure seems like a lot of folks who have tattoos want to discuss them.

We also share common stories people about others' tattoos. We pity the really bad ones, the misspellings, the Japanese kanji that was supposed to say "strength" and says "tofu" instead. People pity women's sex-reference tattoos in a different way. The "Curves Ahead" sign on a woman's hip, a cat adorning a shaved pubic mound. Men's stupid tattoos are still seen as a sign of wild abandon; women's are seen as bad judgment or an advertisement of loose morals (which somehow is still synonymous with an interest in sex). When I was growing up, I was told explicitly that a woman with a tattoo was damaged goods. This went beyond bad judgment. My mother, for instance, assumed that a tattooed woman had been dominated by criminals somehow and probably was one herself. That type of damage—like the permanence of a tattoo—was irreparable. She was to be pitied. It's so interesting watching my eighty-six-year-old mother nowadays, in summertime public places where young women with tattoos are obviously middle– and upper-class fashion hipsters. The distaste still shows on her face. When times change, values move more slowly.

People also like to discuss whether or not someone's entitled to have the tattoos they have. It's possible, though, to critique a Hawaiian pattern on a tourist's arm but fail to critique some of the more "bad-ass" renderings of weapons by those who have not seen combat or even religious symbols by those who are not devout. My friend has a large radiant Mother Mary on his forearm—think of the image of Mary on devotional candles in Mexico. His version, however, has pronounced cleavage. She's a sexy Mary. Or maybe kinky Mary, in her religious robes. My friend is not Mexican and not Catholic, but maybe the image would be all the more odd if he were one of those things or both. In any case, no one's ever accused him of cultural appropriation, though the tattoo is certainly a form of that.

Sometimes, planning a tattoo itself can take the place of the actual rite of passage or depth of connection or sense of responsibility one wishes to commemorate. Many guys with tattoos commemorating their children are not paying child support on time or accustomed to leaving work to pick up a sick kid at school. These newly widespread adornments are not unique in representing superficial attachment, however. The wedding ring is a symbol of commitment and sacrifice, but, no matter its cost, the relationship can still be a mess. Though the tradition of wearing wedding rings likely dates back to pagan Romans, the idea that the engagement ring must contain expensive diamonds is the result of marketing within the last century in the United States. Diamonds aren't particularly rare, and, in order to boost their sales, advertising associated them with romance, engagements in particular. Celebrities were prompted to kindle the flame, and suddenly the rock on someone's finger is a measure of the love. Not really, of course.

Similarly, the tattoo is a thing that can be purchased, and, once the pain of placement is endured, the relationship with it's prompting event is just history. The story marker allows for the public display of accomplishments that may or may not have required lasting trans- formation in one's life. A vacation in which one swims with dolphins and feels utterly transformed by awe for the natural world might be inscribed by a tattoo of dolphins, leaping in sunlight rather than any sort of action toward habitat preservation for those animals or even an enduring relationship with nature. The tattoo becomes the event, and the wearer need go no further than to create the story with which to describe the image. And then, we who hear those stories think we've learned something profound about the person. In many ways, the admonishment of something being "skin deep" is true of modern tattoos.

I'm not arguing for or against tattoos (or any other form of body modification), rather questioning what might prompt actual commit- ment and serious reflection, if not painful (often prideful) marks on our flesh-bodies. I don't know. Polynesian familial tattoos embed actual relationships and accountability into the skin. Others who know the code can read them and know to which family and activities an individ- ual belongs. For the culture that initiated tattooing, perhaps prompting accountability was part of the point.

In addition to the gravity of cultural appropriation, tattoos have become but one way we claim association with values based on consumerism. We'd do well to attend to an actual depth of connection and follow-through with responsibilities—such as child-rearing and environmentalism.

I have another friend who recently announced her desire to get a new tattoo (she already has a few) to commemorate her decade of living with chronic illness. She wants to commemorate her strength, survival, and warrior-nature. I'm happy that this will mean something positive for her, not only a celebration of strength but a source of it as well. I'm glad for her tenacity. And then I was puzzled that she was considering images of strength and bravery from a culture she had visited for a few months last year. As much as she loved that trip and it nourished her in positive ways, I wondered about whether images from that culture actually serve the purpose of committing to a positivity that's more than skin-deep.

Sure, it's easy to turn away from images in one's own culture; they're both personally laden and potentially boring. Much as people often find religions other than the ones in which they were raised more "pure," it may be easy to see "exotic" images in a better light. The question of cultural appropriation is more important in some instances too. When a culture has been colonized and those who look like the colonizer feel entitled to use their images, there's reason for concern. Perhaps it's a mark of maturity—or at least impulse control—to recognize that we needn't choose everything we like, simply because it's available to us. Perhaps maturity comes from returning to what one has been given culturally with kindness and interest, rather than seeking outside. When we grapple with the difficult and inane, we may ultimately find peace with what previously vexed us.

The gravity of one's interrelationship with culture and appropriation and privilege can continue the mission of becoming a fighter or a sage or a traveler or whatever the thing is into which one wishes to evolve. Rather than defending our decisions, we find it within ourselves to listen for others' meaning too. This is one way to heal the damage that white supremacy does to those who take it for granted that all images, words, and rituals are available to them, without responsibility.

Mostly, I just wanted my friend's journey toward her own strength and well-being to be true—something more than an imagined connection with mythical strength, translated via magical thinking and an artist's needle into a wearable talisman. I hope my friend finds strength itself, not just a symbol of it. Maybe that's too much to expect from a tattoo. Maybe that's the point.

Really, whatever she chooses will be fine. It's just skin. The tattoo will be both a reminder and a lesson, as with all the body experiences. It will be something that has a meaning to her, and that meaning may or may not be shared by those who view it.

My ex-wife tattooed my portrait on her leg before we even met. We'd been in correspondence and discussing the topic of portrait tattoos of sweeties, and then she did it. It was a lovely tattoo. Most of my friends asked some version of "Is that a little weird?"

I mean, we were "dating" in the modern electronic sense, but, yeah, not really "involved" in the traditional, depth-of-connection sense at all. I glibly countered that no, considering her relationship with tattoos, it wasn't weird at all. Just a picture. Look, I said, showing friends a photo, I'm right next to a bird and the number six.

My friends feared the tattoo was proof of her "falling too fast" or perhaps proof of mental instability. What is sometimes seen as a commitment is really just a symbol of commitment, in much the same way a grand wedding doesn't always herald a stable marriage. Our relationships to our bodies—and their illustrations—can similarly be profound or skin-deep.

It turned out that my own relationship with the ex-wife was in fact an example of how vows can be just words—even when they speak of a long-term bond. As tattoos can be, the marriage was but a fleeting image, despite the legal and emotional process heralding a deeper commitment than mere dating.

We fool ourselves if we believe these symbols can replace deep, transformative experiences that change us and continue prompting us to evolve. Something more is needed than a commemoration like a wedding or a tattoo. Strength, commitment, and connection require attention and constant renewal. They're visible in a different way and usually don't require an onlooker to ask "so, what's that mean?"

They already know.

17.

LETTING THE BODY LEAD

I went back to my regular doctor as soon as I could after having the baby. My need for an obstetrician had been unplanned, and I never liked him much. He told me to stop eating grapes because I was gaining too much weight. What a dumbass.

Maybe my regular doctor was a dumbass too; how would I have known? Sometimes, it's enough to like someone. Doctors often don't know what they don't know. Well, that's everyone, but as a group they're rarely into finding out they could be wrong, uninformed, or ill-informed. I'll tell you why I liked him. He paid attention to my situation, not just my medical chart, from the get. I wasn't yet twenty years old, had already left a marriage to a soldier, and was being treated for high blood pressure. I had student insurance.

"Was your husband violent?" he asked me gently and quietly, when he was doing my first physical examination, pap smear. He was kind. "Do you have any injuries or previous problems I should know about for your care?" I shook my head.

"Can you afford this medicine you take?" He asked as he wrote a refill for my blood pressure medicine.

"Can't afford much." I shrugged, tough-like, and he nodded. Without pressing conversation, he smiled and said, "You just come here for it then." He pulled me into his office and at first I thought, damn it, this old man wants a blow job for drugs. But that wasn't it. I'd known too many other creepy old white men, but he wasn't that way. At least not right then. At least not with me. "Open up that big purse," he said with a laugh, and then he poured in thirty little sample boxes of my medicine—about a three-month supply. I laughed along and didn't say any more. *Goddamn. An ally. I'm one charmed fool.* That's what I thought.

He also did needlepoint. I stereotyped him immediately when I saw so much of it hanging on the walls. I imagined his little old wife, stitching away. My mother did needlepoint and tried to teach me as a child. She put my first effort in a frame, though it was no masterpiece. It went fine for a while, diagonally up from the bottom left edge, but then in the top right corner, things just went to shit. Who knows why I finished it? Obviously having lost all clue of how to do the thing, I stitched on, every which way, like you can't believe a person would persist.

When I asked, he said it was his hobby. His little old wife might've been a capoeira master, for all I know. Stereotype-busting ally doctor. I've been hoping for another like him ever since.

"What did that guy do to you?" I spread my legs, and he had a look. I showed up with my little bald baby in his pale blue padded carrier as soon as I was done with the obstetrician's official postnatal care.

"No wonder you're saying this still hurts. I could've stitched your perineum better with my eyes closed. But then, I'm pretty good," he said, motioning with his head toward a needlepoint mountain lake scene on the wall behind him.

"I wish you had," I said, rolling my eyes. I was healed up, but penetration sex still hurt for a year after my son was born. Good thing there are other kinds of sex. Good thing there are other kinds of pleasure. That's what I figured. Of course, I was hoping I'd heal. I was hoping there was still more to learn about the sensations, sounds, and subtleties of my body than I knew at twenty-one. The pregnancy made me think there was more in store. Wow, morning sickness. No matter what I thought I was going to do, I could be hugging the toilet with no warning. That baby had taken over and made me a host. Who knew that was coming? I figured I'd better stick around because it might be something great.

The birth was an entire new universe of pain. I kicked a nurse. Pop. Right off the end of the bed. Putting her hand inside my vagina to feel the diameter of my cervical dilation was not the right thing for her to do. A quick shove with my free foot.

During the sexual abuse of my youth—even then—I knew I shouldn't shut it down because more information was coming. That's a thing people do: shut the sensations down because of the shame or the horror or the pain. Nope. I'd tell myself, *just notice everything so you can sort it out later. Because later, you'll still be here, but he won't. Just make sure later you're around to sort it out.* That's what I did. I made sure.

The doctor said, "I could cut this again and make a cleaner incision, but with so much scar tissue to trim away, it might be tight and tender for a long time anyway. Probably six of one, half-dozen of the other just letting it heal and become supple again on its own. The body is resilient." I nodded. On that we agreed.

I was big and strong when I started seeing that doctor. Probably an exercise addict, truth be told. I had stopped starving myself, though, and that was a healthy choice. I was a fat kid, and what does this dingbat culture do with fat kids? Starve them, shame them. Because that's helpful. After years of childhood starvation at the hands of doctors and teachers and family members, I took up the task myself. There was something good about having made it my own personal mission to starve myself thinner (which never fully worked, by the way). The good thing was, once it was *my* mission, I could choose to put that task down. I'm not saying it was easy, but I finally did it. Put it down, leave it and walk on. Keep talking, fools. I'm walking. It took a few years of practice to make it stick, and that social noise was (and is) devastating sometimes because I sure got fatter than I ever was before all of that dieting. But here's the thing: my body felt good. It felt good in movement. It felt good in sex. It felt good in sunlight and water. Keep talking, fools. I'm walking.

"Why doesn't the exercise make me thinner or get rid of my high blood pressure?" I asked the nice doctor once. He shook his head and said, "To lose weight, I think you'll have to eat less, but you know. Maybe you're just the size you are. And the blood pressure? Well, you're soon going to be strong enough to kick everybody's butt, but maybe you need less stress." I nodded and listened because no doctor had ever talked to me with that much gentleness and curiosity before. Not since, either.

He handled my cracked nipples gently on that first postpartum visit too. I wasn't making enough milk. The baby nursed relentlessly and wasn't gaining weight very quickly. I told him about the chunk of meat that fell out of my vagina two days after the birth. Plop. Into the toilet. I couldn't tell quite what it was through the blood and mucous-streaked water.

"That was probably a piece of placenta, which would inhibit your milk from coming in properly. Your obstetrician should've made sure it was all out of there, but since he was drunk when he was sewing up your tear…" He smiled with tender sorrow at his own humor.

Relief from pain is a phenomenal high. Feeling seen is a great comfort.

When the baby was finally out of my body, I felt as if I had spectacular cosmic power. I couldn't have walked, but whatever. My baby's father was there having his magical moment with our new child, and the doctor was busy doing whatever he did between my legs. I was just being magnificent for a little while. Totally magnificent. Then exhausted like a motherfucker. Mother.

The nursing was painful. Every time the baby latched on, my shoulders tensed, but the coaches at La Leche League said I had to learn to relax, so that's what I did. My life became one long exercise in getting out the boob, putting the boob away, getting out the other boob, putting the other boob away. I was committed to nursing, and the paradox of my existence was that I needed sleep to make milk, but without enough milk the baby wouldn't sleep. Meditate through the pain, the baby's frantic sucking. Relax my shoulders, steady my breath. Calm my mind.

Then, when it felt like pulling, rather than sucking, the relief came. The sucking sensation turned into a pulling sensation and I could see the baby's throat moving, swallowing milk. I could feel a release through my chest that wasn't the same as a muscle letting go, but close. *Holy shit, there's still so much to know about this body,* I thought. *Sensations I can't even name. Look what it can do.*

My son's father wanted to taste the milk, so he did. I tasted it too.

No big deal. He didn't ever drink. Maybe he would have if I'd been making enough for the baby and then some. I don't know.

It was ten years after that, with a different lover, that I first offered my breast, as I had to my baby—only not like that at all. I can't say why I did it, except that my body decided it was the right thing to do. She didn't freak out, but then, she was pretty pervy to begin with. Still, that's intimate and then some. It was absolutely the right thing to do.

It's a different orientation, body to body. I was seated and told her to lie across my lap, her chest to my belly. I held her head in the crook of my arm and told her to relax. I guided my nipple into her mouth, wider, suck and hold. Sometimes she held my body, sometimes my breast. This is not how people normally behave in sex, and we were totally having sex. But then, how people behave during sex is often proscribed and absurdly stylized. It's influenced by gender norms and media and pornography. We become actors trying out for the roles of our own lives, even while we're fucking. There was no model for this thing I did. It wasn't like sex, until it suddenly stopped being me telling her what to do and became her doing it. It wasn't like sex, until something released and it became a profound erotic connection. It was definitely not the same thing as nursing a baby.

Of course it wasn't the same as nursing a baby. She was a grown adult. My lover. And not even into thinking of herself as a baby. Some people are into that, but no, she was the opposite almost. She was part he, all adult, but part rebellious child; human. We are each a combination of human traits. The mother and child and the uncle and the teenager and the old person, the withered body leaving life. All of us, everything. We just don't act like we know it.

People freak out about this sort of thing because they can't understand versatility. Ohmigod! You were nursing her like a baby! That's kind of creepy, right? Or really sick? Like, were you hot for your baby? No, I wasn't. It's like suddenly no one can wrap their heads around breasts being both sexual and for babies' nourishment. Like that's a new idea. A lot of people are so screwed up about boobs being for babies that it seems weirder to see a woman nursing than a woman sticking out her boobs so dudes can look at them, jack off on them, use them for something that has nothing to do with her pleasure. I'm telling you there was a very particular kind of pleasure in feeling my lover relax in my arms, warm skin against mine, viscous cunt-slip still between my fingers.

When do men's bodies ever do anything as amazing as all of this? Nearly never. That's when.

The thing is, I'll bet they could. They just don't because big and strong, protect and pay, fuck and squirt is all that's in the script. Most people don't know how to put down their social scripts. Men can lactate, for instance. We all have the same equipment, but when do we ever hear about that? The whole male-female thing is one of the ways language makes us real. Obviously there are more than two genders, shapes shift. Obviously we contain multitudes. We are damaged by limited expectations and don't even know it.

Humans can hold their breath long enough to deep-sea dive without an oxygen tank, but that doesn't mean most people do it. We don't feel capable. The body and the mind and maybe something beyond both all need to agree to things in some kind of language most of us don't speak. My friend used to run long distances. I mean the kind of distances that don't seem possible: down one side of the Grand Canyon and back up the other side, fifty miles, without stopping. She said her breath and heart made some kind of synchronized movement pact and she somehow got light and went along. We don't have language for all the things we can do. Of course not. We have bodies right this minute that are capable beyond our belief and mastery.

I know that I can make even the hardest, loveless lover feel love when she's at my breast that way. I know that I can impart wordless wisdom and compassion through the experience of my breast. It's a direct transmission. I know that very few are willing to accept this gift. Fewer know what to do with it.

We can rediscover what we've previously known with alarming acuity. Damage is not forever. We can discover what we've never known with gratitude.

The difference between consensual sex and rape is enormous yet superficially can involve the same movements of body against body. Huge numbers of men don't believe they've raped someone, even when that someone says they have been raped. Sure, lots of men know they're raping, but many more say they didn't do it even when the women say they did. I believe their idiotic disbelief because I've seen how easily men dismiss women in conversation, talk over them, don't notice them if they seem unattractive. I've seen the ease with which men focus on a desired outcome and tune out all the external noise that others might call information about the situation. I've seen that socially and politically and in families. Of course it happens with sex too. It'd be strange if it didn't. For so many girls to know that "the shoulder push" is just how a guy tells you he thinks you should suck his dick, entitlement and lack of communication are the norm for both girls and boys, men and women. The fact that so many girls will just go suck a dick because they feel the push means there's a crisis in how we conceive of pleasure and comfort and collaboration. The social expectation of a goodnight kiss is worse than the expectation of a handshake at the end of a date. A blow-job, however, is a really gross thing to do if you don't want it with every fuck-urge in your body.

Of course, that crisis could be informational. A catalyst. You are capable of more than you can even imagine. I know this is true. Your body can lead you. Pleasure is the guide. And if we don't pay attention, if we force connection or forget that every body deserves pleasure, harm is amplified.

Boobs are fat. That's mostly what they are. Big boobs, when naturally occurring, are big sacks of fat. Your first relationship of comfort and sustenance, if you were breastfed, was fat. You were too young yet to know that we live in a culture that hates fat. The trauma of birth is profound for both mother and baby—the most stunning pain—and what healed each of us from the trauma, most likely, was being pressed against the fat of a body that had to change fundamentally to accommodate us. The mother's body tears open and then usually finds love and pleasure immediately afterward.

When I pulled her close to my seated body, so that her chest was pressed up against the rolls of my breasts and belly, when her arm wrapped around my hip and the other held the breast she was sucking, we were having a depth of contact most women never allow a lover to have. Too much fat. Even thin women might worry. Somebody's touching too much fat.

My lovers have often never been attracted to a fat babe before me, and, once the shame subsides, the pleasure of sensation astounds them. It's not better to be fat than thin. All the ways bodies can be are marvelous. And often, when handling another's body, we'll seek out muscle or fat. Capability and comfort. A lap, a shoulder, a bosom, a strong arm. When my lover first let herself relax onto my body, after sex, she said, "I had no idea how pleasurable it would be to feel your body holding me like this. I can't imagine ever being with someone thin again." In the moment of pleasure, we let go of other possibilities. This is the only moment. Of course it is.

I nodded and stroked her head. It's the kind of epiphany-sensation I never want to disturb too soon. I get it. I like holding my lover's body too. I'm still being born every day into new body knowledge, new pleasure and pain in my aging body, the secret wisdom of new lovers, coming to me with their gifts and prompting my giving in ways I didn't know I had to give. It's still happening, breath by breath, calming my mind, forming around pain and releasing into stillness, into joy and gratitude.

18.

THE BODY IS NO FICKLE MACHINE

It's the kind of vegan burger shop you find in a big city or maybe an eccentric small town. I'll bet Marfa, Texas, has a vegan burger shop—shakes, fries, burgers, and of course kombucha too, just to prove a bit of nutritional consciousness. Everything made vegan, likely with a side of information about the evils of factory farming or harming animals.

I'm a fan of eating some of the stuff one was raised with, even as one's ethical palette evolves. When I stopped eating meat more than thirty-five years ago, the tuna melt was the last thing to go. It represented comfort to me, and I couldn't easily release. I get it. Food is not only nourishment; it's part of our life force in a far more complex way.

But, wow, those vegan burger joints are not about nourishment in the nutritional sense. This particular one is full of twentysomething, tattooed darlings along with occasional aging weirdos—like the wife and I—the people who end up accidentally cool just by making our own agendas and sticking to them. Those youngsters tend to cleave toward the greasy burger when they're not vegan too. It's cultural; it's what we eat; it's a moment in the life cycle when most people's digestive tracts are pretty forgiving.

Some folks will always feel good eating that stuff. Weird that we tend to associate Big Macs and Cokes with fat people when the majority of those who eat them aren't fat at all. Ditto with the vegan variety, but then people rarely associate being vegan with being fat, and that's surely possible too.

My wife and I each had a burger and fries. Pretty good really, but salty and greasy. I find my digestion doesn't complain if I have the kombucha along with it. A bottle of collaborators, that's how I think of those kombucha organisms. *Get in there little buddies, do your thing.* I have a warm feeling toward the intestinal helpers as I'm swigging it down. Could that be part of why it works? I dunno.

So, on the way home, the wife—a newly minted, rather high-horse vegan—says to me, "I just feel better when I eat that way."

"What way?" I say. I can hear the mild superiority in her voice, so I figure she doesn't mean salty greasy fast food, since that's supposed to make one feel not so superior at all.

"You know, no animal products. Cleaner eating," she replies.

"You call THAT clean?" I say, a bit incredulous, and then I notice her belly noises, her uncomfortable shifting in the passenger seat as I drive.

"Can you drive a bit faster," she says to me. "My gut's not right and I'm going to have to…" Her voice trails off in that *you know what I mean* kind of way. And I do indeed know what she means, better than she does, I think for a moment, because she is carrying on talking about the superiority of eating as we have just eaten while her body is putting forth quite a powerful counter-narrative. And I'm sort of glancing over at her midsection while she's talking because, wow, things really don't seem okay in there. I check in with my own gut but I just feel mildly heavy, not ready to explode out the exit. I glanced at her face, twisted into a grimace, as she kept talking about "clean eating" and urging me to drive faster. Does she really not know that she's in pain?

When I was a kid and I'd eat a bunch of candy, my mother would say, "You're going to make yourself sick."

I tried on that idea, but it just didn't fit. I'd check in with my belly, and, no, nothing felt sick at all. I mean *at all*. I have a pretty strong constitution generally, and eating too much of something didn't really ever make me feel ill. My friend used to get a "tummy ache" when we were little, and we generally ate the same things. Her mother would put her to bed, and I had to go home, if I was visiting. I wondered sometimes if she didn't just want to lie down or be alone and couldn't quite muster saying so, but it was probably just that my tummy was different. We lived in different bodies after all.

I did, however, realize from all that *you're-gonna-get-sick* prattle that I could check in with my body, feel my feelings, and realize whether or not I was sick. I could also check in and see whether or not I had emotions about something. Sometimes—often—I would still choose to hide them, but I knew they were there. Straight up, the *Free to Be You and Me* book by Marlo Thomas that came out in the early 1970s (and then became a play performed by my third grade class) was definitely not just feminist claptrap. I learned a lot about feelings and how to be aware. That is to say, I learned the basics, which was a lot more than some of the adults in my life seemed to know. Often, they didn't seem to actually know their own feelings either, even when their agony seemed ready to overwhelm them.

Everyone knows both the truth and its opposites as true. It's possible to shut the body out of all negotiations as many children do when they learn that their bodies can cause them social ridicule. Social ridicule comes as a result of appearance or behavior or even bodily functions like farting when and where you shouldn't or getting caught picking your nose.

There are different rules for boys and girls, of course, for men and women. I'd like to think that the multiplication of gender means that there will be fewer rules for all, but it might not go that way. We might just make up rules of social decorum specifically for nonbinary folks too; time will tell. Nearly everything a boy can do with his body is excusable, downright laudable—all the functions like hunger and farting and fighting and sex and fighting. Oh, not crying, though, not emotion. Even when it seems like their physical excesses are showing, boys get a pass. The only time fat is a problem on a boy is when it makes him look like a girl. Fat butt, fat thighs, fat face on a boy—oh, hell no. But a big torso, belly, or shoulders can be overlooked. Nothing ideal, like having a six pack and bulging biceps, but it'll be okay. Not boobs though. Good lord, not boobs.

How does one sort out the food, emotion, meaning, health, and bodily response conundrum in such an environment? We've all had our wires crossed and soldered young in a culture that equates female "goodness" with the ability to constantly say no to two of the body's most urgent desires: sex and hunger. We have to reclaim our body sovereignty, for greater health and vibrancy. Luckily, there are a million ways to do it.

I was talking recently with a researcher at an academic conference. We were at the bar, where a lot of the real talk goes down, and she'd been discussing the strangeness of living in poverty her whole life and now doing research on/with women in poverty and how immediately they assumed she was different than they were because of the initials after her name. Even with the PhD, she didn't have anything like a full-time job, and so she was still poor. I know that story by heart, tending to gravitate toward the outsiders, being one myself, so after a while I said, "Right, so I'm buying you dinner."

She said, "No, no, not even."

And I was like, "Dude, you just got done telling me your grant for this conference works out to about $3 per day for food, so duh."

She was the kind of woman I felt comfortable calling 'dude,' especially after we'd been talking the long hour like we had. She let me buy her a second glass of wine and when my pizza came I foisted a slice on her. She was doing that humble-nervous-submissive thing a lot of new academics do when they think you're more established than they or they know your work, which seemed to be her situation with me. She may have been new but was not young, almost my age, which added another layer onto our interaction, a comfort. But she wasn't totally comfortable.

She pointed to the pizza on her plate and said, "I'll eat that when I come back from a cigarette." I nodded and watched her walk out to smoke. When she came back, she stared down the plate like an enemy for a moment (I thought I made that up at first) and then ate the pizza, in three or four big bites, raising her hands at the end like she'd finished a race and exclaimed "There! I've eaten dinner!"

I laughed and said, "Wow, I didn't mean to force you." She nodded, then turned pensive.

She looked me in the eye and said, "You know what? Sometimes I prefer being hungry at this point in my life. I mean, it still hurts just as much as it did when I was a kid and we didn't have enough food, but now it gives me a sense of accomplishment too. I'm nearly fifty. I feel powerful. And I'm still poor, so hey. Why not enjoy it? Funny how something that hurts can feel good after a while, right?" She ended with a shrug.

I said, "Yeah, I totally get that." Because I did. I *had* sort of forced her to eat dinner. I got that part too, just a little too late.

Hunger was different for me as a kid. We had plenty of food, I just wasn't supposed to want to eat it because I was fat. I was supposed to be virtuous and resist food. I got so much praise for not eating that it *did* feel like virtue not to eat it. But then not being allowed to participate in all of the deliciousness and beauty and community that food is and represents to humans also made me so angry. I sometimes ate "too much," whatever that means. It made me feel defiantly alive.

I mean, seriously, what does it mean to eat too much? Well, it means more than the body wants in a given moment, or things that the body doesn't like. That's from a corporeal perspective at least. But food is complex. Can one ever really eat too much for the emotions or for the intellect? People gulp down more celery and kale than they really want too because the mind says it's a good idea. Too much for what part of us? We are not our metabolisms, that's for sure.

I never felt bad eating candy, like my mother threatened, so was I eating too much? If the body is like a machine, then I was using the wrong grade of gasoline, but the machine still operated without trouble. If you follow the wisdom of popular and medical culture, only the rational mind should be engaged in deciding what goes in. Don't let bodily and emotional urges run amok. Convenient that those are the urges associated with the feminine and women are the ones most blamed and shamed for body nonconformity and size transgressions.

The truth and range of human experiences is more complex. Pain can feel like celebration. Starvation can feel like virtue. Good feelings of sweetness and fullness can turn to shame. We may be more than our bodies, but we are also our bodies. Machinery we aren't. Energy in, energy out as a straightforward equation? No way. In addition to basic body difference in metabolism, we relate to food in different ways that promote health or illness. I was buying fancy cheese once, with a line of ash laid through it. Yeah, ash. My friend said, "is that even good for people to eat?"

The cheese monger said, "Look, when it comes to rich, fancy French food, it doesn't matter if the body's meant to have it. Made with enough love and artistry, in small doses, you can digest anything."

Sorting it all out is going to require gentleness and tenacity. The repetitive trauma and body disassociations some of us have endured prime us for untangling things in the culture that others don't even see. We have to get ourselves a bit sorted before we have something to offer, though. We just have to keep adding new circuitry until those messed up pathways aren't worth traveling any longer. We find ways to get our perceptions to match up with our experiences while still holding compassion for every kind of combination in which awareness comes forth. There's information in every single interpretation. How beautiful it is to find pleasure in deprivation and pain because pleasure affirms life. We can hold every bit of beauty loosely, gently, fiercely, and keep celebrating the deeper joys of becoming allies with our bodies, which is to say, with ourselves.

As with my wife's body/mind schism when coming home from the vegan burger joint, we don't always hear all the voices of our immediate experiences. Fair enough. Just by breathing and coming into the body's experience, it's possible to sort out the feeling *in* the body from the thoughts and feelings *about* the body. And then, with practice, one can learn to hear each voice separately while still enjoying the chorus. Sometimes we can help each other too, by using kindness or just plain witness. The more we practice kindness toward one another, the more consistently we can give it to ourselves when needed. It's totally possible to think one thing and feel another. Just accepting that makes one more open to the mystery of these human experiences. Sometimes the body remembers or hears or understands something the mind can't grasp. Sometimes it's best to just wait, listen, eat the French fries if needed, and let the lesson come in its own time.

Until every response we can have toward our bodies and lives becomes allowable, we struggle. Like how I felt both virtuous when starving and angry about being diminished led to shame and a gritty fortitude for both dieting and bingeing. It's possible to love the anger, love the desire for virtue, love the choices that lead to survival as a path to greater peace and pleasure. It's possible to put down shame, again and again, every time you notice you're clutching it like a soldier with a trumpet leading the charge for cultural convention. Just put it down. Enjoy a bit of birdsong. Enjoy a bit of silence. Try to find a little peace, no matter what else is happening.

19.

I'M NOT THE ONLY ONE WHO LOST FAITH

I learned years later that my mother went to the church for guidance. Why wouldn't she? She was part of that congregation, and her parents attended as well. It's only natural that she should bring a difficult family problem to her community of faith for input ... but wait. The problem involved her family and the church and potentially criminal behavior that could cause scandal. Was it still appropriate to rely upon the elders of the church as guides?

When I was in my early twenties, rebuilding a long-broken relationship with my mother after years of tension and distance, she told me that she went to the church for guidance. She told the church elder, that I, her daughter, had accused the pastor—also her husband, my stepfather—of child sexual abuse. He advised her against pursuing the matter because I probably made it up. After all, they'd never had any allegations or complaints of sexual misconduct about him from children before. Only from single women or divorced women, and, well, children aren't any more trustworthy than they are.

When I was little, I never wanted to go to Sunday school. I wanted to go to "big church" with my grandmother. I promised not to fidget and to say all the words when I was supposed to and stand and sit according to cue. I loved the vaulted ceilings and stained glass and how the whole building was built in the shape of a cross. The clear windows on the sides of the church let in the light and green from the valley beyond the walls. I felt held by nature in that room, surrounded by magnificence. Sunday school was in a stupid classroom. In a basement even. I didn't find that inspiring, and I was told I was supposed to find church inspiring. I didn't want to settle for lessons. The big church made me feel God.

I loved the sound of our pastor's voice as a child too. He was sometimes booming and sometimes thoughtful, quiet for emphasis. When we all went outside after the service, people stood in line to shake hands with him. I guess we did too, but I don't remember shaking his hand. I remember being eager to get my cup of punch and cookies and lean against the railing out of the crowd so I could watch him yet be removed. He was charming, and, from the responses of the adults I could see at that distance, he was also funny. They seemed struck by his celebrity. He had authored a few books and held the largest congregation in the state rapt each week. That's how I felt too, awed yet familiar. My parents divorced when I was eight; and when my mother announced that she would marry him, I was ten. I thought it was one of the best things to ever happen to me.

I left home early because, after three years of abuse and finding the courage and outrage to accuse him, she looked for guidance in the church (among other places). And then she stayed married to him another eight years.

I found my own way. I learned, through women survivors' support groups and then activism, that others had been sexually abused by clergy and not believed. So many others. Once the shame of sexual abuse is gone and the talking becomes easier, the pattern of who abuses and with what protection becomes very clear. People who are surprised at the data on women's sexual abuse and assault—people who think they don't know women who've been sexually abused—they just haven't learned to listen. Or they protect abusers more than they believe, so no one's talking.

So common and intricately woven is clergy abuse and incest, I found myself on a date a few years back and, without much conversation at all, we realized that our abusers knew one another. They were both clergy. Abuse is a profound experience, to be sure, and also one I learned to discuss and then write about, so that we can all come to see it as a cultural issue that must be addressed collectively. Among other things, my abuse history is a source of wisdom, a source of solidarity with other feminists and survivors. And we are legion.

My family's religion was one of the larger, more mainstream and progressive Christian faiths. What the church elder's counsel offered my mother was a basic misogynist interpretation of how children should be protected, who was credible, what should be believed and when. A lot of children had it much worse growing up, sexually abused in their faith communities. A lot worse. I found my way, both through the personal sense-making of family and faith and also through a sense of social responsibility to talk about incest, to talk and write about misogyny and child abuse. But this essay is about my mother. I'm not sure she has found her way after those events, and, while healing my own life was first priority, I still hope she finds peace.

My mother attended church growing up. Her mother took her every week, and her mother became my link to the church as well. By the time my mother was an adult, she wasn't a Sunday morning regular, though she still counted herself among the congregation.

As a pastor's wife, however, she was dutiful. We lived in the parsonage during part of my youth, and, wow, when they own your house, the parishioners sure feel like they own your time. My mother was gracious (if privately complaining) when church people dropped by unannounced. Around the time of my incest disclosure, my mother's church attendance dropped off, much as mine had around the time the abuse started. I couldn't hear him the same way anymore. Was it that way for her? She didn't force my attendance, and my stepfather didn't force hers.

After the divorce, she felt that church—the whole denomination, it seemed—was no longer her place. To my knowledge, she never attended another service at that church. She didn't even go for my stepfather's funeral. His other wives would be there, and all of those church people. I understood why she didn't want to go. Not to mention, she wasn't invited, though she stood by him all those years. I can't know what horrors the other wives stood by to watch. Chances are, they all count themselves long-suffering.

I gave her estrangement from the church little thought through most of my life. *Sexist hypocrites,* I thought in my youth. *Better she's away from that stuff.* Then time offered a more complex view. My life and spiritual/religious pursuits have broadened, but it seems hers haven't. She watches church on television every Sunday. Early on it was Jerry Falwell, Billy Graham, Oral Roberts. Now she's a fan of Joel Osteen. Her faith is the same, but her faith community is no longer tangible, local. Now that she's past eighty, I'm pondering what she's lost.

In my youth, our church was a place of liberal political pride for me. Jesus was a role model for helping others. The man who sexually abused me also spoke eloquently of Christian generosity. He welcomed draft resisters to the church during the Vietnam War. He was an intellectual who introduced me to Virginia Woolf, even as he seemed to feel entitled to sexual access to all women—and children who looked like women. And the church knew. Of course they did. The church moved him frequently from one parish to another, a strategy I recognize now as crisis management. Keep quiet and we'll take the problem away, only to give the problem to a new community. This is part of how abusers end up affecting so many, across such vast geography at times. The church may not have condoned his behavior, but they certainly stood by him. Just like my mother did.

I asked her recently what her desires were for her own end of life. She became upset discussing it—not just because imagining one's death can be challenging. It seemed to me the hardest part was imagining where I should hold a service for her. She did not want her life remembered and discussed in that church, yet that's where her parents and brothers before her were celebrated. I navigated the conversation as best I could, upon hearing her indecision, but then wept later at her involuntary displacement. My own departure from the church felt more voluntary, and it happened earlier in my life. She had actually tried to stay and found it too inhospitable in the end, even after such effort.

I lost one home but built others. My own faith has become a combination of Buddhist practice and connection to Christian social justice and peace work. I am both at home and still somewhat guarded in Christian settings. Quaker services are most comfortable to me—sort of a Buddhist-Christian combo, to my mind. No one person in authority.

I am thinking of Catholic Worker Dorothy Day's comment on the political-personal schism when she said, "There must be a disarmament of the heart." My mother is aging, and I am wondering less about her armaments against a faith community that betrayed us than about the barricades she has built. She seems to have no weapons whatsoever. She doesn't speak or write as I do about these events. She remains a silent nonparticipant.

Women have not, in large numbers, taken up arms against the misogyny of their Christian churches, but I feel certain many have built barricades. And those barricades protect and isolate them yet leave religious misogyny unharmed. This is the question I hold: how might those who love deeply flawed institutions change them for the better without becoming martyrs to the cause? At the end of life, the possibility of dropping barriers seems simply too much for people like my mother. And too, the fortress is isolating. It's amazing that more women have not walled off both men and churches. But just as my childhood "big church" experiences taught me, there's more inspiring and holding us in awe than just the men talking. There's the light, the green trees, the sway and song of the people. Maybe that's why those televangelists have such a following. They're images on the other side of a glass, still carrying the symbols and words of faith and hope.

20.

WHEN DOES LIFE BEGIN? IT'S THE WRONG QUESTION

Laws curtailing how women manage their bodily autonomy, health, and reproduction are harmful to the entire society. Literally no one is left undamaged by these restrictions, as I will show. They strip those who reproduce of basic human rights and reframe the origins of life as though sperm is irrelevant. Further, abortion policies that allow for medical intervention only in the case of rape or incest are not benevolent. They are established to protect the men who rape and impregnate their children and neighbors. They are meant to erase from the body what the mouth has already been told not to tell.

Further, these policies were never meant for lawmakers and other elites anyway. They're for people who can't afford to get their kids or their wives a good illegal abortion. Abortions have always taken place. Throughout all of time and for a huge range of reasons. Ending pregnancy is part of life and deserves support, not punishment.

Asking when life begins focuses people on something ineffable, perhaps unknowable or at least variable from person to person. It's not the right question. A person capable of having an abortion is already a life in process. That person is a decision-maker—the only one tasked with the very complex task of stewarding the contents of a uterus that may or may not contain human potential. If abortion involves sloughing off some unwanted cells in the interest of health and well-being, or if abortion involves ending a life, that decision belongs to the people to whom (and inside of whom) those things are taking place.

You might be surprised to learn that, as a culture, we have already decided this—and if it weren't for the politically precarious position of women (or anyone with a uterus), this issue would be far clearer.

We already have laws about bodily autonomy on the books. If I am in a terrible accident in which I will die if I don't receive a blood transfusion—and your blood matches mine—no one can legally compel you to offer your blood to save my life. Your blood is part of your body and cannot be taken from you without your consent. I have given blood and carried a child to term and given birth; giving blood is no big deal, whereas carrying a child to full term and giving birth was one of the most profoundly transformational and life-threatening events ever to happen to my body. Those without the ability to gestate and give birth can't know, and that's only one of the reasons cisgender men should not be the only ones involved in making decisions about women's bodies. They lack firsthand experience of what life is like with a uterus and aren't listening very well to those who have them. Even worse, they're trying to codify women (and people with uteruses) as being not fully human under the law. In essence, they are currently trying to declare that women are exempt from the same bodily autonomy we've already decided, as a culture, that all humans share, even after death.

If, in that accident, you died and I needed one of your organs to live, a doctor would not be able to give it to me unless you had expressly given your consent as an organ donor before your death. You wouldn't be using it, and I would die without it, and still a doctor could not give it to me.

It bears mentioning here that, though we're discussing abortion, some of the legal changes being attempted to limit health care options for women can affect women without uteruses as well. The arguments used in these policy discussions rely on historical precedents about women's worth that cause many people to not notice that something dire and nefarious is happening in this realm of body autonomy. Though the gender binary is a social construction and there are men and nonbinary people who have uteruses and can give birth, these new, increasingly restrictive abortion laws are not specifically aimed at curtailing the rights of transgender, intersex, and genderqueer people. Sadly, there are other efforts aimed at forcing or denying medical care to members of that community. Seventeen states still require some form of surgical intervention before people can legally change their sex on public documents, and some states require sterilization of those seeking to update their driver's licenses, birth certificates, et cetera. (We're not alone on this in the United States—the same is true in countries like Japan, Finland, and Romania.) So, as we discuss abortion, it's important to note that public policies are still very much formed around an assumed gender binary and, as such, are grounded in the historical precedent that women should be controlled by men. When I say women and men, I'm mostly referring to cisgender women and cisgender men in heterosexual relationships—because that is what the laws I'm discussing also assume.

Life and death are complex, emotional issues and should be discussed with reverence to the great mystery and respect for one another. We will all face death. The problem with the current politics and policies around abortion is that they are less concerned with the true meanings of life or death and are much more about deciding whether women are a special, lower class of people who deserve to have their right to bodily autonomy revoked. Should we be forced to save the life of another person—if indeed an embryo or a fetus is a life—by sacrificing our bodies against our will?

I've never had an abortion, but I have had a few miscarriages. I've also given birth and parented a child to adulthood. Many have miscarried in the process of becoming parents or on the road to remaining child-free. Some don't even know it's happened. It's a natural thing for the uterus to get itself ready, for the body to occasionally struggle while figuring out the business of baby-making. Gestation is a huge job that requires so much of a person's physical body. (I'm commenting just on the body here, because, of course, the person's well-being is also involved in myriad other ways: emotionally, spiritually, and financially, for starters.) The old saying among mothers "for every child, a tooth," refers to the fact that our bodies sometimes lack the resources to make a baby and keep all other systems intact at the same time. I didn't lose any teeth, but then I had health care and access to good prenatal vitamins.

When I miscarried, I didn't feel that I was losing a baby. I was losing the possibility of a baby. For some, that's devastating. For me, I was losing the possibility of what might've been in some alternate reality. The same is true with abortion. Sure, there's often more volition involved, but it's still a loss but also a gain. I didn't realize how profoundly my life and my body would be overtaken by carrying a pregnancy full term, having a child—until it happened. When I miscarried, I gained the ability to continue going to school each day, rather than hugging the toilet, too sick to move. I gained the ability to keep working and walking farther than a few blocks on sore and swollen feet. To me, my miscarriage was a clot, a collection of cells that fell into the toilet, after some sweaty cramping. That's how it happened both times. One time, it was very painful, the other, not as bad. I may have had more miscarriages during that window of pregnancy in which most abortions are performed and just didn't know it.

These experiences are not standard, not stable; neither are people's feelings about them. We can either make loving space for the diversity of human stories and experiences with the potential for life, the beginning of life, or we can shut off some people's stories as inappropriate. We can offer shame and censure rather than learning about the full range of human experience. There is already a precedent for women not sharing their experiences with sex, reproduction, and the end of pregnancy. As a culture, we don't acknowledge what we're missing. We blind ourselves to a full understanding of life and death and institute policies based on that ignorance.

Most men are not aware of—or learning about—the full range of human experiences. They are also certainly not listening clearly enough to women, or we wouldn't be in this political mess about abortion. If these men better understood the process of impregnation, gestation, and birth from the perspective of those around them who endure it, it would be clear to them in screaming Technicolor: Even when the life of a viable fetus is involved, the same bodily autonomy that allows someone to decline giving a bit of blood, or a corpse from donating an organ, would place decision making only with the person whose body might possibly be used to potentially save the life of another.

If men knew how often women endure harassment, feel fear, have been raped or molested, and experience pain during sex, it would be a different world. Of course, there would still be women who don't favor abortion or who hold fringe beliefs about the autonomy of the female body, but we'd be discussing those views in a more robust environment, rather than taking pro-and-con sides on a topic that has many, varied perspectives and interpretations based on immigration, race, religion, ability, labor, et cetera. We never even get to these myriad disaggregations because that different world is so distant from our own.

Not only are men socialized to not listen to women's experiences, women are socialized to not share the details of their sexual and reproductive lives, particularly with men. It's a nonverbal, largely unconscious pact men and women make not to share the specifics of horrible experiences with one another. We each think we're protecting the other from our pain, which sets a precedent for not sharing fully about our joys and other nuances of human emotion and experience. I think we need to acknowledge it far more often: men are socialized to be hard and stoic, and women have been socialized to like it. Even more, women have been socialized to enjoy cracking the male façade, becoming the only person with whom he can open up, just a little bit because usually he keeps things to himself. We say "poor guy" when we discuss male emotional constipation, but, really, many women have learned to see it as evidence of love.

Similarly, though women are thought to excel at emotional expression, women are discouraged from sharing the depth and breadth of our experiences with sex, our genitals, our pain, our harassment, our victimization, and our pleasure. We don't learn to share with our partners about our sexual pleasure because we are socialized to believe it isn't important. Men often don't want to hear too much about their female lovers' sexual histories because women are seen as more valuable to a partner if they are more chaste. Men are supposed to be better for their sexual experiences, though so little is expected of their expertise with the female body.

Very little has been expected of men, historically, when it comes to gestation and childbirth. Relegated to hospital waiting rooms or pubs while midwives did their work, men in the last few centuries have been mostly uninvolved with the birthing process. Things are changing for sure, yet those precedents remain.

Despite men's lack of involvement with gestation, their role in impregnation is pretty clear. Gabrielle Blair explains how things could be different if we centered this fact in her article "Men Cause 100% of Unwanted Pregnancies." It seems so obvious, yet we don't discuss it because pregnancy has been so powerfully framed as a women's issue for so long. It feels normal to make the uterus responsible.

Truly, 100 percent of pregnancies are caused by sperm, and men have the ability to control sperm. If there's an ethical question about whether abortion is okay, controlling sperm would be the clearest way to go. Plenty of sex does not result in even the possibility of pregnancy. When sperm is not present, there will be no baby. We've culturally enshrined male orgasm to the point where we never discuss the possibility of "orgasming irresponsibly," as Blair calls it. To my knowledge, no one has ever been accusingly asked, "Why did you let your sperm get anywhere near that woman knowing the potential consequences?"

What if two people needed to file for a license and set a clear intention before sperm could even legally make an appearance between them? Sex wouldn't be regulated, of course. Just sperm, due to its ability to create a whole person and put another person's body and life at risk. Imagine. Perhaps it seems dystopian, but it's far less dystopian than forcing the person with the uterus to hold on to and nurture that sperm because it may become a human someday. We need to acknowledge sperm as the root cause of pregnancy and move discussions forward from that point.

While there are politicians at work to curtail in alarming numbers the freedoms women can enjoy, there is also one example of the government enacting eminent domain over men's bodily autonomy: involuntary military service. Though America is not currently drafting men for military service, men are still required to register for selective service within thirty days of their eighteenth birthdays. Many don't. It's been more than a generation since those registered have felt the fear of being called to fight.

While many rules curtail what humans do with our bodies (using certain drugs, for example), the draft seems to be the only one that forces only men into potential peril against their will. Abortion bans and selective service are supported by people across the two dominant political parties in the United States, but more Republicans than Democrats support abortion restrictions and bans.

How is it not completely absurd for Republicans to say they want smaller government but then spend so much time repealing human rights and liberties? How are people within the party not questioning this contradiction? I claim no allegiance to either party and can only speculate. What's clear is that, in one instance, women are rendered inconsequential when it comes to making decisions about their bodily autonomy. They are considered secondary to a clump of cells with the possibility of becoming a baby. In the other instance, bodies—men's—are being elevated to the status of a weapon. They are considered too important to the nation, in a particular moment, to be governed by individual interest. No one is saying their will is inferior, only that the perception of their superior strength (compared to women, who are not required to serve) is needed for a common goal. When men are drafted, their bodies are being called to service, but their value is not being called into question.

The social assumptions on which these policies suspending bodily autonomy rest are very important. We need to handle this issue directly: men are thought to be of greater use as weapons, women are thought to be of greater use as baby-makers, but the practical reality is that men are often more successful at exerting their will as sovereign individuals. Even when they dissent, though shamed, they have not faced the kinds of punishments currently being devised for women and their doctors in regards to abortion. Sure, draft resisters sometimes faced punishment during wartime. In 1977, however, hundreds of thousands of draft resisters were pardoned by President Jimmy Carter. Selective service is a related though dissimilar phenomenon that we'd do well to discuss further.

When it comes to making public policies about bodies and the pregnancies that can result from sex, our ability to discuss sex and pleasure privately, among ourselves as individuals, is quite relevant.

I currently see no evidence that most policy makers are able to discuss sexuality with poise and clarity, let alone acknowledge the current patterns of intimate gendered interaction in the United States. They are unfit for their work in policy-making due to ignorance and inability. These are topics that concern all humans, the future of society, the safety of children. We need to stop worrying about when life begins and start building the skills to discuss how life unfolds for the vast majority of us already living.

If we find it too shameful or embarrassing or untoward to talk about how fewer heterosexual women orgasm during sex than their male lovers, or the fact that men are more likely to be rapists than women, or that more women experience pain during intercourse than men, or that more men are prone to violence (and using sex as a form of violence) than women, how can we expect rational policies to emerge?

Imagine a world in which people come of age, feel physical yearnings, and begin to explore with one another with a mutual understanding of lust, respect, and a curiosity for what those feelings bring not just in their own bodies but in also the bodies of those with whom they're exploring. This scenario would come with an understanding that sperm is dangerous to those who want to remain child-free, because in a scenario of mutual respect and curiosity, of course, everyone involved would take responsibility for the outcome of their actions. If young people placed more value on prioritizing female pleasure, anatomy, and safety, we'd be a lot closer to this ideal. Girls don't masturbate nearly as often as their male peers, and many boys aren't interested in seeing, touching, or tasting the female sexual anatomy either. It's becoming more common for men to clandestinely remove their condoms during sex with women too. The practice is called stealthing and is discussed among men and boys as a good trick to enhance pleasure. It's irrelevant to those who do it that it also renders consensual sex nonconsensual and puts the woman in danger of pregnancy and possibly death.

From the time heterosexual teenaged boys and girls get together to explore sex, social programming has already led them to believe that the most important aspects are a male's pleasure and a female's desirability. The widespread prevalence of female emotional discomfort and physical pain isn't part of mainstream conversations and is rarely researched. In fact, according to a study reported on in *The Week*, "30% of women report pain during vaginal sex, 72% report pain during anal sex, and 'large proportions' don't tell their partners when sex hurts." We rarely discuss the research that shows that respectful exploration in which people have good first sexual experiences does exist in one group: girls who have sex with girls. When girls have sex with boys, they have already learned that their primary job is to be hot. And hot girls don't talk about real human needs. That might be a bummer for the boy.

Of course, despite social conventions, people of all genders and sexual orientations are capable of discovering that sex is totally magnificent when everyone's engaged and coming (when they want to, of course). But that discovery is countercultural because the idea that women's bodies exist independent of men's needs is also countercultural. So common is the dismissal of women's daily harassment, assault, and pain, as is the significance of our pleasure, that we don't even see it as a baseline when we discuss public policies affecting those of us with uteruses.

While I am completely certain that the miscarriages I had did not involve the death of a baby, something different happened when I got pregnant and stayed pregnant. When I gestated my son's body, I experienced the beginning of life inside me as an ineffable miracle. At some point, I was aware of not just having "something going on" inside of me. I was aware of a person there. Experiences with pregnancies differ a great deal; this is how it was for me. During those last few months of pregnancy, I came to know my son as a distinct and definite human being. I feel I've known him longer than anyone else in this life has known him. I knew him while he was still in my body.

Would I have given my life for him at that point? I might have. I'm glad it was never a question of who lives and who dies: him or me. But, should it have come to that, my right to bodily autonomy and the ability to make the best decision for me—and for him—would've been more important than ever. I'm grateful we both survived his birth and that I know him as a full human being, now with his own son and his own set of human challenges in his own autonomous life, which he guides with aplomb.

I do know this: if abortion were safe and easy to get, there would be so very few people who delay the opportunity to have one when they know they need or want one. We would not be discussing "babies" as often; it simply wouldn't be relevant. We'd be discussing cells sloughed out of the uterus and only the potential for a child having been lost. That same potential is lost when people decide not to have sex, or chose to use protection or birth control or get a vasectomy. There are many realities we could be living but are not, every day, in so many ways.

For those who make the difficult choice to abort later-term pregnancies (rare though they may be), we must offer support and careful listening to their stories; they can teach us a lot about one of the many trials of being human.

We all have the right to make decisions of consequence. Just as individuals who choose to withhold an organ or a blood transfusion from someone whom they could've helped, those who choose to have an abortion have made a deeply personal decision about their life and bodily autonomy that deserves the same level of respect. As humans, that's what we must each learn to do.

21.

AT LEAST I'M A THOUGHTFUL LIAR

When I teach a yoga class, I step forward into a lunge with my left foot, but I tell the students to step forward with their right foot. That way, when they look up for an example, I am a mirror. It seems like we're doing the same thing.

I don't actually think I'm moving my right leg when I tell students to move their right legs. I feel my left leg. I acknowledge my left leg. And then I say, "step forward with your right leg…"

Most of us lie or manipulate or fail to frame an issue for clarity when it suits us. And because of the social stigma on lying, we act like we're not liars. Sure, many draw a line about outright lies that we will usually not cross. We hold conflicting views. It's a bad thing to be a liar. Most would agree. And we also hold a deep and persistent understanding of how others lie, when to expect it and how to be careful. But what about ourselves? Some lies are so habitual. Because we cannot bear to define ourselves as liars, we erase our knowledge of what we're doing. We don't keep our right and left sorted. We act as if everything is just as we say it is.

The first time I heard my ex-wife explicitly tell a lie, it was a whopper. We were dating at the time; I don't know if we'd discussed marriage. Even the marriage we eventually had, according to some people, was "a lie."

I joked that we were getting married so we could continue dating. Marriage—at its base a legal contract—is laden with so much cultural meaning. Everything about a marriage is supposed to be true. True love. Total fidelity. No lies between you ever. It's easy to fold one's spouse into the shroud of secrecy most maintain about their own lying. That's why the culture maintains clichés and idioms like "she was the last to know" or "he just couldn't see it coming."

You already know the cultural edict. In order for a marriage not to be "a lie," it must be about two people making a lifelong commitment involving monogamous sex and family and tenacity, forgiveness, compromise and hard work. When I spoke of our marriage and acknowledged the fact that we were of different national origins—surely a factor in our decision to marry legally rather than simply cohabitate—some dismissed our love for each other and desire to form a household together. "A marriage of convenience," they said. I was astonished that people would speak this dismissal directly to me. So strong is the mythology around marriage that deviating from the standard story makes one's honesty suspect. I thought I was telling a more complex truth, to acknowledge all of the story.

When I heard that first big lie, I was visiting my sweetie for a few weeks—it's the only way to "date" when you live on separate continents. Her housemate was having a romantic relationship with another close friend who was married to yet another friend. They lived in a small town. This was no small or secret affair within the household. During my whole visit, we could hear them having sex just upstairs. The woman sometimes didn't go home at night. And she didn't tell her husband she'd be away. When she did communicate, all lies. The distraught husband, also a close friend to my sweetie, called her cell phone one night—the illicit couple just a room away—and asked her straight up. "Is my wife sleeping with your roommate?"

What would you do? You know and care about all of the parties involved. You know that there is deception, worry, and the couple has young children. You have complex feelings. My sweetie chose to say, "No, they're not having an affair." And then she went on to bolster the lie that (to my thinking) would clearly be found out. She didn't just tell a simple lie like, "I don't know." She went all in. In the course of her elaborate convincing, she said, "Don't you think if they were having an affair I'd know about it?"

Ouch. At that moment, I knew that someone who lied that boldly and easily to a friend would lie to a lover as well. She would, most assuredly, lie to me. I did not keep this from myself. And though I acknowledged it, I decided to carry on with her anyway.

We live in a time in the United States when we acknowledge that politicians lie in order to continue doing their jobs. Hundreds of jokes belie our cultural understanding, and politicians even sometimes campaign on the platform that they can be honest in the role exactly because they are not politicians. We love that, even though, wait. They're running for office. Our daily lives and language constitute a complex web of deceit and doublespeak. Similarly, it's becoming increasingly more accepted that police officers and military personnel will lie "to protect their own." Yet their job is to protect the very people they're deceiving. When these entities investigate wrongdoings such as rape in the military or police brutality toward citizens, we simultaneously expect that justice will be served and that there will be some lying and covering up. Citizen review boards have now been established in many cities to investigate police misconduct because we understand that there is no overriding code of honor in these professions that would make their own honest investigation possible.

Of course, my ex-wife went on to lie to me. Many times during our short marriage. Perhaps my knowledge of her ways felt like a talisman against the gravity of impact.

I told her, after the phone call about her friends' infidelity, how very uncomfortable her words and tone made me. She hung her head briefly and said she felt like a real shit, but she didn't want to get involved.

That's exactly what she'd done, I admonished! Then she said something else with a remorseful tone, but the content was dismissive. She didn't want to feel bad about it. I watched her shake off the whole incident. She agreed with me, superficially, that she should've refused to comment and referred him back to his wife. Lying and then forgetting about lying in order to preserve her positive sense of self had become a habit for her. When a person is nearly fifty, a long-held habit is hard to change, even if one wants to. Not impossible, but difficult. I consciously acknowledged that, in the moment, because I wanted to be sure I was staying honest with myself about the company I was choosing.

I'm a liar too. And I try to choose my deceptions very carefully. I'm not driven toward honesty by religion or moral superiority; it's that I've seen the harm in lying, and I know that my complicity hinders the world in which I want to live. My choices influence others, just as I am influenced by others. Culture-making is a reciprocal arrangement.

I sometimes don't tell a full truth because I want to be kind. Or encouraging. Or helpful. At times, I am far more certain of what is kind than of what is true. Why devastate a student whose thinking and writing may be a bit off by eviscerating the effort? Unless I am quite sure of what needs correction, I focus on what's going well instead and circle back around to complicate and expand on the not-quite-right topics. Teaching—whether it's yoga or writing or sociology or advocacy—has taught me a lot about truth and kindness. I've become a more a humble learner. I mess things up. I feel humbled by defeat in human interactions—especially with those I care about most. This is true at the same time that I acknowledge the truth in how others see me: I'm a better communicator than most.

My ex-wife struggles with bipolar disorder. When we were together, I struggled with it too, and I have read a lot about it since we parted company. She didn't tell me she had a bipolar diagnosis when we got together, nor did she at any point in our cohabitation. She told me about her anxiety diagnosis. She told me she was medicated for depression. Truth is complicated. I don't know whether she knew about the bipolar when we were together and simply didn't want her list of troubles to be too long as we were negotiating a romance. Most of us will try to hide our troubles in order to appear as desirable as possible, early on. Is that lying too—or just image management?

Perhaps she was just so overwhelmed by her own roulette wheel of daily difficulties that she simply forgot that one. That's what she told me later. That seems possible, and unlikely. I believe that mental illness—and the social stigma on mental illness—play a role in her consistent ability to lie and omit and reinvent.

I care about my ex-wife and genuinely wish her well. That's what love is, as I understand it. When things were calm and we were both working and enjoying each other's company, I loved our peace and compatibility. We had romance, love, and sweetness when she was able to see me as an ally. We also had so many difficult times. Every forty-eight hours or so, she'd be angry and manic enough to tell me we were through. She swore it was the end. Every few days. Later, she'd say she never meant it. She went back and forth like that despite my anguish. I told her it needed to stop or I'd have to leave. I stayed until I couldn't anymore and followed through on my threat.

I've often said that writing saved my life. It's a dramatic, artistic thing to say, no? Here's how it happened. I grew up in a family where appearances were very important. I come from beautiful people with beautiful things and magnificent stories. My mother still can't tell a story about someone she's close to without casting the person as the pinnacle of success. She doesn't spend time with anyone who isn't the top of his field, a genius, award winner, a model or athlete.

I was different. I was too fat for the family story and then too sexual—pretty but in the wrong way. When my stepfather began sexually abusing me at age twelve, of course it was my fault. Or it simply wasn't happening. One or the other. Sometimes simultaneously. By age thirteen I was a suicidal drug user with an eating disorder. The only reason I didn't fail the eighth grade was because it didn't fit with the rest of my story. A white girl in a rich neighborhood couldn't possibly fail the eighth grade, so the school fixed it. That's why it didn't happen.

I didn't really want to die; I wanted rescue. I was seriously losing the thread of reality. That is, until I realized that if I wrote down exactly what was happening to my body and in my emotions today, just today, I could go back and read it again tomorrow and know for sure. There'd be a record because I knew I had not lost the truth of current sensation. Thus I rebuilt reality, based on my physical experience, one day at a time.

Yes, I was also writing bad angsty poetry and emotional rants, but it wasn't just "creative" writing that saved my life, it was the simple chronicle I kept of who did what and when. Rereading those entries helped me understand that, wow, my family is fucked up. Lots of people I know are fucked up. Maybe everyone in my whole community is fucked up. Maybe I'm fucked up too. But I am not the biggest, or the only, problem here.

That's how writing saved my life and how my personal investigation of truth-telling began. By age fourteen, I had started paying attention to the truths that emanated from my body as well, rather than pushing them away as most are taught to do. A feeling of stress or fear means I should pay attention. A feeling of ease is a sign things are going well. At fourteen I started reassembling a sense of self outside of my family of origin.

Within that family, during those early teen years, I lied a lot. I lied about where I was going and what I was doing. I lied about whether I was high, whether and with whom I was having sex, whether I'd been to school. This is a familiar "liar's starter kit" for a lot of teenagers. To be clear, I lied for my own benefit.

See how that language works? Given the story I just told, I could've said that I lied to "save myself" and most would feel fine about it. I think it's more accurate to say I lied for my own benefit. That's what most people do. In the moment my ex-wife lied to her friend on the phone about his wife, she was sparing herself from the judgment of those in closest proximity. It can be that simple.

Somewhere inside, I think most people feel that they are lying to save themselves, even when the lies seem utterly inane. When my mother says her new boyfriend is a genius, millionaire, top of his field, she is saving herself. At some point, she felt imperiled and learned that a simple way to breathe easy again was to say something different. Lying or omitting important information is one of the first forms of salvation humans find. Most children learn it doesn't work for long. Either they're not good at it or it has negative consequences. It's damaging to relationships. If adults are there to show them other options, they learn.

There is plenty of evidence, however, that our culture supports the social pact not to discuss common lying, because everyone's doing it.

We even reframe lying as a skill. Think about how often people see lying on one's taxes as "being smart" or "working the system." Think about how easy it would be for most to keep something that doesn't belong to them if a business makes an error. Somehow, lies become a tool for reclamation of what we "deserve." Our personal values both mirror and create culture.

When my son was in seventh grade, he lied about his findings on his science fair project. This became clear as he was writing up the final report to hand in. Perhaps he didn't do the project at all. There were no steps to report, it seemed. In any case, his alleged findings could not be replicated. This was no simple project. His grand lie required a series of small lies throughout the entire semester, some of them to his teacher, some to classmates, some quite public. He couldn't easily come clean and salvage a sense of self. Self is also still forming in the seventh grade. After initially flying off the handle about his deception and telling him that he would march right in that classroom tomorrow and come clean, I reconsidered what it might mean to actually live with a the identity of "liar" at that age, in that venue. He attended a small school, and it's possible that label would be hard to shake. I also knew that because he comes from a queer family—both his parents are gay—he already felt quite other. I paused for a second thought about what this "coming clean" might mean in his situation.

Not to mention, he flat out refused to do what I said: march in there and tell the truth. He screamed his refusal back at me, red-faced, and then ran into his closet and shut the door and cried, angrily thrashing about, as he had done before under dire circumstances. I walked out of his bedroom and into my own, sat on the edge of the bed, and had a few deep breaths. That yoga comes in handy. I considered what I would feel and what I might do in his situation but with my own adult wisdom.

Yeah, I probably wouldn't have agreed to my Plan A either. Plan B, which he did accept, if memory serves, was to create a really quick and shoddy "redo" of the science fair project that very night. Hand it in and live with the miserable grade. If the teacher said anything, he could simply say, "Yeah, I didn't put as much time into this as I should have."

And that would be the truth. A partial, expedient truth. But no more lies. I helped him to log findings in a tabbed binder that night. Something to do with a penny and a little electrical device that he couldn't get to work right. The description of findings sucked. I don't remember what grade he got, and he chose not to talk to me about it any further. I had done the best I could. Lying can be an easy way out. It can also make a real mess.

Sometimes honesty allows for other solutions to emerge—as was the case when my son was at least honest with me about the science fair debacle. The second solution I offered hadn't occurred to him. He was able to maintain a positive image in school despite the failure of that project. He didn't need to take on the label "liar."

Sometimes turning a corner and simply moving on with no more lies isn't enough. My nation, for instance, has created great wealth on the backs of people of color. Sure, slavery as an institution has ended. We have created some legal assurances, such as abolishing public segregation, that help move toward equity. And we do not yet have equity. Culturally, most institutions and many individuals tell the lie that racism is a thing of the past. Paradoxically, African Americans should forget about slavery, but all of America should "never forget" the 9/11 attacks. We are accustomed to carrying non sequiturs unquestioned. As writer Ta-Nahesi Coates reminded us, the debt of racism is a bit like running up a large credit card bill and then vowing not to charge any more to that card. That's a step in the right direction, but you can't then be surprised that the balance you charged is still on the bill. Well, you can be surprised, if you're used to deception and platitudes as a way of life. (We're also still charging on that card, even though we said we shredded it, so there's that lie too.)

I sometimes wonder what would've happened differently if my wife had been capable of honesty about her mental illness. I might have still chosen to build a family with her, and she might have been able to treat me as an ally. I wouldn't have minded a little extra work toward her well-being if she'd been capable of gratitude. Not a big bunch of codependent hard work, mind you, but I have faith in the kind of honest acknowledgement of personal challenges that prompt give and take. As it was, she tried to manipulate me into looking after her, all the while claiming she didn't want a caretaker. Doublespeak and simultaneous impossibilities, just like in my childhood. I started writing things down again, just to keep track, and sometimes I felt like that imperiled thirteen-year-old once more.

I wish my wife had been able to say these things:

I will likely not be able to contribute financially to our household in a significant or consistent way.

My ability to work will be erratic, and sometimes my moods will be difficult to live with. I want to be taken care of through the rough spots.

I will not be able to hold your needs or anything that's important to you in my mind for very long. Sometimes I can be caring and loving. It just won't be according to your timeline; it will be according to my ability.

Would I still have chosen this relationship? Maybe I would have. Of course, if she had been capable of saying those things, a lot would've already been different. We would've been able to strategize together, for starters, rather than each of us feeling that the other needed to be managed for our own survival.

I trust that people do their best most of the time. I trust that people are not assholes for the sake of it; they're assholes because they feel imperiled. They feel pain or fear. We tell stories, craft lies and deceptions because it seems that our survival depends on it. Sometimes it does but far less often than we imagine.

During our marriage, I became tight and pointed, as if she were a problem to be managed. Both my financial freedom and my daily peace were in jeopardy. I wanted ease and comfort so badly. It's laughable to think that ease and comfort can be forced. Neither of us was laughing.

I'm more likely to lie by omission than outright. Outright lying—if one defines it as such—sets off a little buzzer for many people. The line is harder to cross consciously, so we make justifications. But omission? Most of us would call it a lie when someone has omitted something of consequence to them. But it's not a lie when we omit. Then it's just ... omission. Different language and criteria for different circumstances.

When I was a teenager, putting my life back together after separating from my family of origin, it became very important to know, inside of myself, when I was lying and when I was telling the truth. It was important to me to *decide* to lie—to know to whom I would lie and under what circumstances. It seemed to me that all those adults I knew had become so fucked up because they lost track. They didn't even know what was real anymore. They just smiled and made shit up, hid what didn't suit them. Even today, I mark the occasion of a lie, inside of myself, though I lie a lot less frequently. I never want to lose track of the difference between honesty and lies.

To be clear, I feel entitled to create both truths and lies. I respect that others are also entitled to lie. We are each independent variables in our own experiments with life. I would lie to save my children's lives, for instance. No doubt. I might even lie to save myself embarrassment. I don't lie as often to get or save money. Some do. As long as we know where our boundaries are and hold on to an internal map of our actions, then we are at least consciously creating our lives and our culture. If I lie, I will bear the external and internal consequences of that lie.

Honest equates with trustworthy. Sometimes that's too simple an equation. I become trustworthy in a lot of ways, not just by telling the truth. And people who are honest may not always be reliable. Some really just don't want to be burdened by civility. They don't want to think through the consequences of what they say, so every blurt becomes "just being honest." Honesty in all cases is not always a virtue.

Somehow, my culture has decided that all we need to look for to prove righteousness is truth. Our judicial system asks us to swear to tell the whole truth and nothing but the truth. How is that even possible in a stressful situation when we have no practice at it in the day to day? How is it useful to focus only on truth when truth is an "as we understand it" construction?

I was part of a jury selection process recently in which an attorney manipulated the group into saying that they would feel comfortable convicting someone on circumstantial evidence, and that they would feel comfortable assuming intention, without knowing anything about the person being accused. These are not exceptional manipulations; attorneys specifically learn to lead people toward certain conclusions. Is that lying? In a courtroom, it's an agreed-upon process of constructing truth. Truth is a set of agreed-upon outcomes, the product of a process we acknowledge as trustworthy. Total social construct, all of it.

Would I have agreed to a life with a spouse who needed care and could not operate according to a traditionally accepted model of partnership? I might have, simply because I value nontraditional adaptations. We already had a nontraditional relationship because we came from different parts of the world. I'm a good planner. I'm not rich, but I conserve well and find what I need. When I raised my son, he benefited from these skills. Why shouldn't a spouse benefit from them? In a general sense, I believe that people with greater skills and resources should share with those who have fewer. Nations that acknowledge this basic equation in their policy-making are consistently rated as the happiest places to live. Happiness is important to me. Just as a culture needs diverse viewpoints, so too a family might benefit from different ways of approaching things.

I'd like to think that, if she'd actually been able to ally with me, I'd have wanted to help—to set up a life in which we each contributed according to our abilities. Perhaps understanding my support as something other than her failure would've enabled her to feel like a good person. Without feeling a "need" to lie to make her rough spots seem even, she might've felt her own worth, looked at her difficulties with compassion rather than pushing away responsibility when she did unkind things. Perhaps this is just my fantasy.

It took me a while to understand that my ex-wife's urge to help homeless people, often feeding them or following them on the street to help with odd tasks, was very personal. She deeply feared joining their ranks. I couldn't talk her out of that fear. It's right that I couldn't because talk is cheap. She does indeed have a habit of alienating loved ones with vicious words and unaccountable behavior. Those traits don't pair well with not being able to care for oneself financially. If she weren't charming and cute and funny, she'd be out there too. She knows it. And because so much of her life is centered on manipulating outcomes, which parts of "charming, cute and funny" are "true"? I'm not sure many of us can sort out the truth of our character from social expediency. That doesn't mean it isn't worth reflection.

What if none of us had to construct elaborate fronts in order to be respectable? What if we could lie on one occasion—because it seems inevitable that we sometimes will lie—and then learn to tell the truth again as quickly as possible through the support of those who still love and respect us? I'm not sure how that would happen other than individuals practicing it on the small scale. It would require individuals to know the difference between their own lies and their truths—the difference between the truths that arise from our experiences, our bodies, our earnest hopes, and those that arise from social expediency. Awareness is not always enough, but sometimes it is. Sometimes it's a precursor to change.

What if the ability to trust another was built on the ability to trust oneself and acknowledge the manifold traits and expressions of caring, dependability, and love? Perhaps we'd learn to repair relationships rather than throw them away. Perhaps we'd be able to support and acknowledge each other's unique ways of seeing the world. And then we could build public policies based on kindness and the generosity people naturally feel when they have enough for themselves and enjoy the happiness of others. Sure, some of these things are a tall order and a long way off, but trust, caring, dependability, and love are a foundation for something very different than we have now, culturally. I'd like to know what can be built on that bedrock.

I don't understand everyone's truth. I just know that collectively we're not yet telling the whole truth about who we are as individuals in relationships or as participants in social systems. We have the ability to influence our own lives, values, and choices, though. We are creating culture along the way.

That's what's true. Along with so much else.

22.

YOUR FRUIT BOWL IS (REASONABLY) SAFE

I used to steal fruit.

It wasn't really stealing. I never did it at the store. It wasn't fruit burglary. The fruit-taking involved no willing offer, though I was always invited into the home. A guest. How can I explain this?

If I came to your home before, hmm, 2005? My relationship with your fruit bowl may not have been entirely consensual.

Fruit is sort of on offer anyway. It's in a bowl, like candies would be. Nature's candy. Take one. I didn't open cabinets (very often). I didn't rifle through crisper drawers. It's in a bowl in the center of the table, so the arrangement is implied. Grapes are easy. An apple can be picked up and bitten into, no problem. An orange is trickier. I may have once taken a pineapple.

There's a difference between being offered a snack and just taking one, between consuming the apple whilst in someone's home and slipping it into one's bag. I know this. I'm not stupid. I'm saying I'd take your fruit and slip it in my bag. For later. When you weren't looking. That's why it was stealing.

"Can I have that orange?" I said once when visiting someone's house.

"Oh, sure." There was a slight pause. I didn't know the person too well, and I sort of blurted it, apropos of nothing. "Let me get you a napkin," she finished.

"No, I just want to have it, not eat it." I said, slipping it into my bag. No shame. Just desire. See, asking for the fruit was progress for me, so seeming weird wasn't my first concern. Nowadays, I'm usually only concerned about "seeming weird" in hindsight and only in that "I hope I didn't make anyone *too* uncomfortable" kind of way.

Your fruit bowl is never totally safe. Neither are you. Life involves risk. And sweetness. Life involves unuttered offers and many—too many to count—mild transgressions. It's good to have a snack along. It's good to share.

I'm grateful for what you've shared with me.

I have been in danger, endangered, lived my life with danger, and now I am quite comfortable almost all of the time. Certain moments call in strange thoughts, and I do what I can to soothe them as all who've felt threatened will do. Continuing to feel endangered skews one's view of the world. We are all holding some kind of damage. Multiple forms of damage, most of us. Even the relative safety of not needing to protect oneself daily from gender affronts or racial affronts renders people defensive and fearful that their safety will be taken. Victims seem like monsters for pointing out that they have been treated unjustly. As Sarah Schulman explains in *Conflict Is Not Abuse*, feeling superior to others and being traumatized by others can both lead to a tendency to escalate conflict. This is the thing about damaged people. We know how to escalate a little fear. We also know how to soothe fear. Remember that story about which wolf you feed?

Healing is episodic. It doubles back, and trauma breathes again. In certain moments, all things are true, and then progression is linear once more. If you're afraid you might not have enough food later, take the fruit. That fear may be irrational, but you still deserve to soothe it. If you can do something to increase your own peace—if you can allow a friend to nourish your peace, do it. Taking the fruit is better than not taking the fruit. Asking for the fruit is better still.

To be clear, most days I carry my own snacks, or I feel safe in knowing that there's money in my purse and food is available nearby.

It's best to expect that some days, a person will not be able to listen,
or will not be able to respond to you
as though they've understood you
even if they've done their listening best.
It's appropriate to assume goodwill.

Sometimes all a person can do, on a given day or month or year
is to pick up the suitcases from one apartment
carry them down the hall into another,
open a window, think of dawn, consider leaving town
but stay instead.

Sometimes, all a person can do is
carry the suitcases into your bedroom,
hastily push one under the bed,
throw the other on the clean bedspread,
fling it open and let the dirty monsters out.

When I tell you something about myself
I want it to feel important
that I have chosen to share with you.

When time passes between us,
I want it to be filled with small moments
that let me know your tendencies
and tipping points. I want to know
what fruit you like and when you like to eat it.

Sometimes I will help you with the peel,
accept a morsel from your sticky fingers to my mouth,
remind you that the smell
of fermentation coming from your bag
needs tending or there will be flies, infection.
A bad time will come if you don't keep cleaning it up.

I will look into your eyes and touch your hand.

Sometimes, though, you won't let me near.
I will wait, turning to my own affairs
without a bad word about you in my mouth.
I know you think the telling is worse than the truth;
you are mistaken. We can recognize each other,
even save each other's lives in certain situations
then harm each other later. That's why
I have to look after myself.
You should too.
That's why I forgive you. You should too.
You saved me once, and I won't forget that our stories
are printed front to back in the same book,
that privacy is constructed of particleboard disintegrating
in the humidity of teardrops, that our narcissism will not protect us.
There is grace and raw power in admitting
that we are not alone and often guilty.
Touch is important,
as are the fleeting facial feature changes in a real conversation.
I don't need to leave you forever in order to find me.
We need poetic understanding,
reasoning without full form and punctuation,
knowledge without clear criteria.
Sometimes, progress has holes in it,
more breath and fewer words.
Deeper feeling.

Just put it down and look at the water.
Watch the way the waves come in sets
how the liquid eddies, drains from the sand.
There's too much stress in shame.
Get guilty; get grateful; then get up and go when you're ready.
I have been a thief, and I have learned to ask, not take.

I was taught that my hunger was wrong.
I am sorry for how I looked at you
when it seemed like that was your fault.
I am resilient. I have been the sweetest
star fruit in the bowl; when
your hand moved toward me,
I surrendered with every cell.

When I feel properly entitled to take my place and you feel properly entitled to take yours, then we are just people solving problems, making beauty, offering love.

23.

THE SCHOLAR-PERFORMER AND THE AUDIENCE

Using my own body, biography, and identity, I can maintain and extend the human dignities of our time.

I have a body. I have multiple bodies—this one I'm in and each one that I've ever inhabited—the body of a child, a young person, a parent—these are a few. You are looking at all of them through this body. I have a body.

I have a story—a biography that looks linear, but we know how life stories go. So, I have stories. I can tell them in a timeline, sure, but most of us tell stories episodically, as the need for a story occurs. That makes sense. Yes, I have many stories.

I also have identities. I put them on in succession and also individually as the audience or my ego requires. Sometimes my only identity is parent. Sometimes I can be a parent and a teacher at the same time. Sometimes it's hard for my identities to intersect in the same moment. I turn away from parts of myself when I'm wearing certain faces. My identity is not always the same as my story, though often they coexist.

I don't just write about culture. I perform culture. This is important because I'm providing an active model of cultural creation. I am a presence and a process—I can hold conflicting objectives and methods. What I offer as a writer and as a live performer is a constant making-sense.

This is why it's tough for me to do the same performance for too many years at a time. I change. My body changes. The way I understand the world changes. If I'm lucky and diligent, the way I understand the world changes.

I don't have to participate in a process or presence that serves a colonizer. I can stand and write against othering. (Who is the colonizer? The colonizer is the individual or business or organization or government that wants you to conform for some purpose other than your own. The colonizer sometimes tries to convince you that your purpose is the colonizer's purpose. A keen awareness and a gentle process are needed to heal from this deception.)

I am going to expose the lines through which power runs and articulate pedagogies of hope and freedom—open options by which anyone who experiences oppression can confront both culture and individual oppressors with kindness and dignity. My dignity heals others. It is, after all, a compassionate act to reveal how a person is being hurt by holding dominion, holding privilege. Injustice harms all, and our ignorance does not save us from injury.

I am offering politically informed performance ethnography, poetic representations of ephemeral circumstances, because every aspect of human life and culture can be studied. We can know ourselves and the context of our lives but not always with numbers, not always with stories, though these tools serve too. These are the privileged media, and I ask, what more? I use presence, poetry, and breath. There are other tools too.

The tendency to over-theorize, close all the exits in an argument—these are not helpful to the creation of a clear, creative, or evocative presentation. I know that the audience is human first. They enjoy rhythm, connection. They deserve pleasure. Yet I am interested in the terrain between show and tell. I will not forsake tell. I have something to tell.

Though meanings and strategies are fraught with disagreement, we can come to agreeable lines of action that affirm and comfort. I pay attention to what works for people. Every time we concentrate power, essentialize information, specialize too much—someone is left out. I am learning how to use the tools and perceptions of scholarship while breaking down the barriers that the guise of scholar establishes. The epiphanic moments we have about how our lives float in the bowl of culture—race, gender, class, and nation—can be brought to bear on meaning. I offer you possibility, a model for possibility and presence.

I am an entertainer. I believe that action and connection are anti-dotes for despair. I suggest that you heal. I know that we can learn.

Using your body, biography, and identity, you can maintain and extend the human dignities of our time.

You have a body. You have multiple bodies—that one you're in and each one that you've ever inhabited—the body of a child, a young person, a parent—these are a few. I am looking at all of them through that body. You have a body.

You have a story—a biography that looks linear, but we know how life stories go. So, you have stories. You can tell them in a timeline, sure, but most of us tell stories episodically, as the need for a story occurs. That makes sense. Yes, you have many stories.

You also have identities. You put them on in succession and also individually as the audience or your ego requires. Sometimes your only identity is parent. Sometimes you can be a parent and a teacher at the same time. Sometimes it's hard for your identities to intersect in the same moment. You turn away from parts of yourself when you're wearing certain faces. Your identity is not always the same as your story, though often they coexist.

You don't just write about culture. You perform culture. This is important because you're providing an active model of cultural creation. You are a presence and a process—you can hold conflicting objectives and methods. What you offer as a writer and as a live performer is a constant making-sense.

This is why it's tough for you to do the same performance for too many years at a time. You change. Your body changes. The way you understand the world changes. If you're lucky and diligent, the way you understand the world changes.

You don't have to participate in a process or presence that serves a colonizer. You can stand and write against othering. (Who is the colonizer? The colonizer is the individual or business or organization or government that wants you to conform for some purpose other than my own. The colonizer sometimes tries to convince me that my purpose is the colonizer's purpose. A keen awareness and a gentle process are needed to heal from this deception.)

You are going to expose the lines through which power runs and articulate pedagogies of hope and freedom—open options by which anyone who experiences oppression can confront both culture and individual oppressors with kindness and dignity. Your dignity can heal others. It is, after all, a compassionate act to reveal how a person is being hurt by holding dominion, holding privilege. Injustice harms all, and our ignorance does not save us from injury.

You are offering politically informed performance ethnography, poetic representations of ephemeral circumstances, because every aspect of human life and culture can be studied. We can know ourselves and the context of our lives but not always with numbers, not always with stories, though these tools serve too. These are the privileged media, and you ask, what more? You use presence, poetry, and breath. There are other tools too.

The tendency to over-theorize, close all the exits in an argument—these are not helpful to the creation of a clear, creative or evocative presentation. You know that the audience is human first. They enjoy rhythm, connection. They deserve pleasure. Yet you are interested in the terrain between show and tell. You will not forsake tell. You have something to tell.

Though meanings and strategies are fraught with disagreement, we can come to agreeable lines of action that affirm and comfort. You pay attention to what works for people. Every time we concentrate power, essentialize information, specialize too much—someone is left out. You are learning how to use the tools and perceptions of scholarship while breaking down the barriers that the guise of scholar establishes. The epiphanic moments we have about how our lives float in the bowl of culture—race, gender, class and nation—all else—can be brought to bear on meaning. You offer me possibility, a model for possibility and presence.

You are an entertainer. You believe that action and connection are antidotes for despair. You suggest that I heal. You know that we can learn.

24.

DAMAGED, LIKE MY SON

When I was pregnant, I read every parenting book I could find. I read every bit of literature on giving birth as well—artful renderings of the birth itself, of the plasticity of pregnancy, the madness of becoming two. Nothing could prepare me. I was possessed with another human being, and soon it would emerge. He would emerge. We'd learned that the child was a boy, and I had strange mixed feelings about that too for a little while. Somehow it seemed easier to raise an empowered girl than a non-entitled boy. Somehow the boy joy offered by all of the baby's grandparents was comforting, even though it was gross. Clearly, all that reading had done nothing but amuse me during the wait. Still, I'm glad I learned the sex early because by the time he was born, we belonged to each other, baby and I; gender was the triviality it should be in the best of worlds.

Choices were all the rage in the parenting literature of the late eighties and early nineties, so I wrapped my tendencies around the concept of choice. When our son was small, sometimes choices sounded like "Do you want to stop hitting your cousin on your own or shall I help you stop hitting her?"

I think his dad was a bit more indulgent than I was, but we both had a good sense of social responsibility when it came to our son's impact on others. If he became loud or cried excessively in a restaurant, for instance, I'd lean down and whisper emphatically, "Look around you. Do you think any of these people in this restaurant want to hear you cry while they eat their meals? LOOK at them!" The choice was to be quiet or be snatched out into the parking lot where I would stand still and unentertaining until he popped his thumb into his mouth like a little cork and I said, "Are you ready to go quietly back into the restaurant?" He'd nod, squeezing out the last tear.

I felt like a tyrant at times. Whatever you might be feeling is secondary to the responsibility of public decorum. *Good god, am I turning into my mother?* I wondered. Her sense of public decorum allowed for no bad behavior, no poorly fitting clothes, no inconvenient truths, and no low-class behavior to be shown. Few emotions were allowable in private either.

No, I just wanted him to think of others. I wanted him to understand that we are accountable to the reasonable comfort of those in and outside of our family. *Just don't be an asshole,* I thought, as I shot my toddler a glance on a crowded bus. And like children the world over, he cottoned onto expectations and was appropriately rewarded with love and foolishness on a regular basis.

At least I hope he mostly felt love and ease. As an adult and a parent himself, he seems to have a hard time putting his needs first—or even equal—in the family he has built. Or is that just his mother's perspective? I know I didn't expect perfection, but sometimes he felt like I did. The only time my son was ever a student in one of my writing courses, a painful part of our family dynamic squeaked out as I reviewed my expectations for our class culmination performances. I talked through my list with the group and at one point I said, "It doesn't have to be perfect, but I want to see you give the audience your best." And he blurted, "That means it has to be perfect." It was the sort of too-loud blurt that belies a joke; he had been hurt by my expectations before.

I overheard my son's voice once—he was past toddling but still under the age of five—in a writhing pit of brightly colored plastic balls at a children's dining establishment where noise was the norm. There were a dozen kids in that thing. The entrance was a slide, and the exit was a low chute opposite the slide. Kids had to get from one side to the other, and they weren't all polite about it. There was my little boy, trying to help a child who was wailing, being continually kicked in the head by other children coming down the slide because she couldn't get out of the way quickly enough. He was trying to tell the kids in the slide to slow down, watch out. She was probably too little to be in there, but who could extract her from the undulating cage? Those children were left to their own devices in that thing, and my son seemed to be the only one who wasn't a candidate for *Lord of the Flies*. He was becoming agitated as he pulled her arm, too small himself to do much good in all those balls. He was getting, louder, saying "She's just little! You have to help anyone littler than you! You just have to. She's littler than you. Stop pushing! You have to help her!"

I weep now at this memory of his earnest, helpless pain. From the moment I knew that I was having a boy child, a white American middle-class boy child, I knew that I had to teach him to pay attention to others, to pay attention to his social position and to set his compass on compassion and accountability. We can't always rely on what "feels right," after all. In an environment where easy pleasure too often trumps complex pleasure, privilege can turn us into supremacists who don't even realize we shun others. I know this. And still, it's easier sometimes to avoid the parental pain of watching a child feel helplessly responsible, as he did that day in the ball pit.

A bit older, maybe nine, my son commented on another mother and son as we sat in a shopping mall dining area. There was a big yellow plastic Ronald McDonald melded into a garish park bench. A woman sat on the bench while her son—maybe four years old—climbed all over the clown. Well, that's what it's for. The kid was yelling things like "Look at me" and also licking the clown, straddling the shoulders, sliding off, and climbing back as the whole situation became slippery with spit. It was an unsavory spectacle.

My son watched for a while and said to me, a bit smug, "Tell me you never allowed me to do that sort of thing as a child." And I shook my head, also feeling smug. "Never." I replied.

I mean, what were we up to there? Good clean liberals out among the rabble, I suppose.

It's even hard to watch our children struggle when they are not helpless, when they have simply messed something up and need to work to fix it. Much as I want him to understand that pleasure can come from the gratification of hard work—I need to keep learning that my broken heart, when he struggles, makes me stronger too.

In seventh grade, the day before his semester-long science fair project was due, it became clear that he couldn't complete the assignment. He'd gotten lost somewhere in the instructions and started faking it, months back. Or I don't know. Maybe he just didn't want to do it. In any case, he had a crisis on his hands, and when I realized he'd just been making shit up, I was livid. I yelled as he glowered on his bed with the binder and all its blank pages around him. I demanded total honesty in front of everyone the very next day. He flat out refused.

Finally, I realized that I probably wouldn't be able to do what I was demanding of him either. Heroic honesty might not have been humanly possible at that point, and all I really wanted from him was a solution that demonstrated personally integrity. No more lying. He hastily assembled something to hand in and received the miserable grade that project deserved. The most he told other kids was "It didn't work." And then he changed the subject.

Parenting changed me forever. Of course it did. It's a big part of one's life that's devoted to the daily care of a child. Both his father and I were devoted in a very daily kind of way. I'm glad for his father's influence in our son's life. He had a hands-on-daily dad. Most kids still don't see men that way.

It changed me because of the time and effort involved and also because I kept having to put myself and my values in his position. When he was in high school, I went to the mat for him in a meeting with his teacher and the principal when he was accused of plagiarism. I debated righteously for his innocence, and there was a split second in that meeting when I glanced at him and saw guilt on his face.

Oh shit, I thought.

Maybe I had become over-invested in that campaign, too fervent to uncover the truth. I didn't win either. Well, I sort of won. He took Fs on all three papers in question, but he was not expelled. I asked him years later if he'd actually plagiarized those papers. I mean, what did I see on his face that I read as guilt?

He said he'd plagiarized parts of one paper but not the other two. That moment of guilt came up when, in the face of my impassioned rhetoric, he saw his teacher start to cry. She had been doing the best she could, he thought. And she was partly right but mostly wrong. He did feel guilt, but at that point he thought we were all too far down the road to retreat.

I didn't even remember the teacher's tears.

Part of what's haunting about parenting is always wondering if I've done the right thing, or enough of it or too much of something else. There's no escaping the fear or inadequacy and no way to prepare enough for the task. We did the basic things in delivering him to adulthood without family members hitting him or having sex with him. I yelled more often than I like and sometimes I was emotionally absent, depressed, or anxious. I always came back, though, as soon as I could. I'm not perfect, and, because he treats me with far more grace than I sometimes treated him, I don't think my son expected me to be perfect.

Some parents set the bar pretty low, for sure. Higher than their parents set it is good enough. I never thought of it like that. I was keenly aware that it's largely mothers who raise sexist men who become the leaders of tomorrow. I didn't want to contribute to that. Of course I wanted him to know I had his back, but not at the expense of him learning about responsibility and interconnectedness. The paradox of protection sometimes kept me up at night.

Learning to be accountable to others may not be enough, but it's something good. Learning not to leave others on the battlefield just because you can make a speedier exit without them may seem like archaic honor, but the kernel is that community matters. An ability to take a few deep breaths and then come back to civility won't solve everything—in fact, sometimes it'll hurt—but I believe it leads to deeper peace in the sum reckoning.

My son is damaged too, in a world where his mother's life has made her vigilant about how he understands his privilege. Make no mistake, though, an awareness of this world's complexity was a gift, when I was able to give it. He is growing up past his own obstacles and mine, finding what sunlight he can enjoy, shading others, cultivating strength and resilience, offering oxygen, beauty, and his own unique interpretation of the human spirit.

He's damaged but not like me.

REFERENCES

Freire, Paolo. *Pedagogy of the Oppressed.* New York: Continuum, 1970.

Maor, Maya. "Becoming the Subject of Your Own Story: Creating Fat Positive Representations." *Interdisciplinary Humanities* 30, no. 3 (2013), 7–22.

O'Donohue, John. "The Inner Landscape of Beauty." Interview with Krista Tippett. *On Being* radio show, February 28, 2008.

Olsen, Tillie. *Silences.* New York: Feminist Press, 2014.

ACKNOWLEDGMENTS

I'm so pleased to have published a second book with AK Press. It's been wonderful working with Charles, Zach, and Suzanne. I appreciate their skill and dedication to the values the press upholds. I'm honored to be in their company and the company of other AK Press authors.

Thanks are due to all who saw earlier versions of these essays and offered response. That includes the writers of whom I requested feedback and, significantly, those who heard me read aloud or responded to earlier versions in print. I don't create in isolation. My thinking finds its way in relationship, and while it's not possible (or desirable) to please everyone, I want these ideas—embedded though they are in my stories and experiences—to be legible and useful to many. My assistant, Rebecca Rubenstein, is a constant help. In addition to those I hope forgive me for their omission, let me name smarty-pants Lucy Aphramor, also Jennifer Niesslein, Laurel Hermanson, Raluca Albu, Erin-Kate Ryan, Rye Gentleman, Samantha Johns, Wendy Smith, Amy Kilgard, and Mary Robertson. I appreciate your astute assistance.

Thank you to my son, Caleb James Dark Westberg, whose stories I am also telling here. He has not always been comfortable with hearing essays that include him, and he has always been generous in understanding that some of his stories are my stories too. They are also cultural stories. I have learned a great deal from the way he navigates the social world.

I want to thank the Black Lives Matter movement. This book is about possibility and capability, particularly born of first hand experience with trauma and marginalization along with surprising interrelationships. Though I most often deal with intersectional identities and how hierarchy based on appearance and identity damage us all—and this very much includes racism—white supremacy in my country deserves a specific mention. The sustained and insidious nature of racial terror in the United States has infected all of us. Some lose their lives, others their humanity.

If you believe (as I do) that unconscious biases will warp even the best intentions, then we have to be constantly vigilant at washing that poison from our cells. This is true for everyone but especially for those of us with white privilege—because otherwise we do harm and then feel wronged when someone points it out. The Black Lives Matter movement helps to keep me on *my* path. In particular, I thank the movement for highlighting and encouraging women's leadership, for highlighting and encouraging Black intellect and strategizing, for highlighting and encouraging Black joy and ingenuity, for highlighting and encouraging intersectional approaches to liberation. We all benefit from these efforts. I benefit, and so does my work. Endless thanks.

I accept that my work fails, and I will keep doing my part. I'm committed to creatively discussing painful topics while inspiring hope and illuminating ability. With practice, I hope to do it more consistently. I'll continue to hone my skill and effectiveness at writing and creativity. In some ways they are separate pursuits, wedded in service of expressing an actionable vision. I hope all people become liberated in ways we can't even yet name. I pledge myself to do better and offer gratitude for all who help me see my way, though growth can be challenging. May we come to see both joy and conflict as part of the package marked "freedom."

Lastly, writers need time, space, and community in which to write. This book benefited from the Creative Connections retreat. Some of this book was written at the Eastover Artists Residency, and some at Dickinson House. The rest was written in my living room, where I thank the ancestors, the sea, land, and sky for the life I have every day.

Kimberly Dark is a writer, teacher and storyteller, working to reveal the hidden architecture of everyday life so that we can reclaim our power as social creators. She's the author of *Fat, Pretty and Soon to be Old*; *The Daddies*; and *Love and Errors*. Kimberly is a sociologist who believes in our responsibility as social creators. Art is one way that we find and re-forge the vast and intricate connections between self and the social world. When personal sovereignty and community accountability connect, beautiful things happen. Kimberly teaches writing at places like Cal State Summer Arts and Corporeal Writing, and she offers workshops and retreats for do-gooders to do better, on topics like unconscious bias and conflict resolution. Learn more at www.kimberlydark.com.